XF-103

Mach 3 Stratospheric Interceptor Concept

Hugh Harkins

Copyright © 2019 Hugh Harkins

All rights reserved.

ISBN: 1-903630-87-8
ISBN-13: 978-1-903630-87-7

XF-103

Mach 3 Stratospheric Interceptor Concept

© Hugh Harkins 2019

Centurion Publishing
United Kingdom

ISBN 10: 1-903630-87-8
ISBN 13: 978-1-903630-87-7

This volume first published in 2019

The Author is identified as the copyright holder of this work under sections 77 and 78 of the Copyright Designs and Patents Act 1988

Cover design © Centurion Publishing and KDP
Page layout, concept and design © Centurion Publishing

All rights reserved. No part of this publication may be reproduced, stored in a retrieval system, transmitted in any form, or by any means, electronic, mechanical or photocopied, recorded or otherwise, without the written permission of the publisher

The publisher and author would like to thank all organisations and services for their assistance and contributions in the preparation of this volume

CONTENTS

	INTRODUCTION	vii
1	MX-1554 AND THE PERCEIVED SOVIET BOMBER THREAT	1
2	1954 AWI REPUBLIC MODEL AP-57 DESIGN ITERATION OF SEPTEMBER 1951 – PHASE 1 DEVELOPMENT	9
3	XF-103 (AP-57) DESIGN ITERATION OF JANUARY 1954	19
4	XF-103 RESEARCH INTERCEPTOR DESIGN ITERATION OF JULY 1957	37
5	GLOSSARY	47
6	BIBLIOGRAPHY	49

INTRODUCTION

Conceived in the late 1940's as a high speed, high altitude air defence interceptor and developed through the 1950's as a Mach 3 interceptor capable of operating against Soviet strategic bombers in stratosphere and possibly extending toward the mesosphere, the Republic XF-103 (Model AP-57) was an unsuccessful entrant in the USAF MX-1554 competition that fielded the Convair F-102 Delta Dagger interceptor. Post-MX-1554, the XF-103 took on the mantle of a research program to prove technologies applicable to a future generation mid-supersonic – Mach 3 – interceptor. However, like the later North American F-108 Mach 3 interceptor concept, the XF-103 was ultimately doomed due to cost and a looming redundancy facilitated by a shifting strategic threat in the shape of the intercontinental ballistic missile, which was in its infancy when the XF-103 program was cancelled in 1959.

This volume looks at the genesis and development of the various iterations of the Republic XF-103 from program inception through cancellation in 1959. The volume is supported by photographs, technical drawings, renderings and planned performance charts from the contractor and intended operator.

There is a deliberate switch from metric measurements to the fore and imperial measurements secondary in chapter one to imperial to the fore and metric secondary in subsequent chapters. This has been done to ensure 100% accuracy in primary measurement reporting from respective designer/test organisations, whereas secondary measurements may, at times, be rounded to the nearest cm or kg.

1

MX-1554 AND THE PERCEIVED SOVIET BOMBER THREAT

The Republic XF-103 was an ambitious 1950's American program to develop a Mach 3 capable high altitude interceptor aircraft to counter the then perceived threat from projected Soviet supersonic capable strategic bomber formations operating within the stratosphere – atmosphere layer commencing just above where the troposphere ends, ~14.5 km, extending to an altitude of ~50 km – and possibly extending to just below the mesosphere – atmosphere layer commencing at an altitude of ~50 km extending to ~85 km. The fear of attack (from 1949 the unease increased as the Soviet Union became a nuclear armed power) against the United States by Soviet bomber aircraft led to interceptors assuming a prominent role in CONUS (Continental United States) air defense as the world moved toward the bipolar superpower stand-off that commenced in the years immediately following the end of World War II in 1945. From the late 1940's, air defense of North America had assumed an urgent priority. By the early 1950's, several subsonic turbojet powered interceptor designs – Northrop F-89 Scorpion, Lockheed F-94 Starfire and North American F-86D Sabre – were in service and the development of supersonic interceptors was being urgently pressed on with.

The first step toward fielding a new high performance interceptor for defence of the CONUS against the projected mid-1950's Soviet long-range bomber threat was the issuing of the ADO (Advanced Development Objective) of 13 January 1949. The major requirement for the new interceptor – referred to as the 1954 Interceptor in reference to the projected in-service year (1954) – was that it have superior speed and operational ceiling performance than that estimated for the next generation of Soviet strategic bomber aircraft (Knack, 1978). The USAF (United States Air Force) issued a RFP (Request For Proposals) on 18 June 1950 (Knack, 1978) for the MX-1554, which called for an interceptor that could attain a speed of Mach 1 and an altitude of 15240 m (50,000 ft.). In October 1950, whilst the airframe contractors were finalising their MX-1554 proposals, Hughes Aircraft Company was awarded a contract for development of the MX-1179 ECS (Electronic Control System), which would be incorporated into the MX-1554 (Knack, 1978).

The deadline for MX-1554 proposals expired in January 1951, by which time six contractors had submitted a total of nine separate proposals, three of which came from Republic Aviation. The only other contractor to submit multiple proposals was Lockheed – two proposals – with single submissions coming from Chance-Vought, Convair (Consolidated Vultee) and Douglas. Three proposals – one each from Convair, Lockheed and Republic – were selected to go forward to the mock-up stage on 23 July 1951. However, before long the Lockheed proposal was dropped, leaving Convair and Republic – the future F-102 Delta Dagger and XF-103 respectively.

Figure 1.1. MX-1554(A) Republic XF-103 (AP-57) design iteration of 1954. NMUSAF

Both MX-1554 proposals were to utilise the Wright J67 turbojet, but the Convair proposal was initially to be powered by the Westinghouse J40 turbojet as airframe development was ahead of that of the engine. Under J67 power it was projected that the Convair MX-1554 would be capable of attaining a maximum speed of Mach 1.93 at an altitude of 18898 m (62,000 ft.) (Knack, 1978).

Although the competition was still officially ongoing it is widely accepted that the award of a letter contract to Convair on 11 September 1951 was a de-facto declaration that the Convair proposal had been selected as the MX-1554 service interceptor and would go forward to serial production, barring some catastrophic technological program setback. The Convair MX-1554 suffered a myriad of development problems, which delayed service entry until 1956, the build-up of operational F-102 squadrons being swift – some 25 ADC (Air Defense Command) squadrons equipping with the type at the peak of service in the late 1950's. Convair built around 1,000 F-102's (NMUSAF).

THE THREAT – ACTUAL AND PERCEIVED – Conceived in the climate of tension and fear that was the Cold War in the 1950's, the XF-103 was developed at a time when the threat of Soviet strategic bomber attacks against the CONUS was greatly exaggerated. By the early 1950's, the Soviet Union had a fledgling long-range bomber fleet in the shape of the Tupolev Tu-4 (NATO reporting name 'Bull') four piston engine bomber, which could strike contiguous CONUS targets on one way missions and targets in Alaska on return missions. The detonation of the first Soviet atomic device in 1949 had changed the geostrategic climate enormously. Release of an RDS-3 atomic (nuclear) bomb from a Tu-4 bomber at the Semipalatinsk site on 18 October 1951 (MODRF) proved the nuclear strike role for Soviet Long-Range Aviation. Development of a viable intercontinental delivery system for atomic warheads would elevate the USSR (Union of Soviet Socialist Republics) from a multi-regional superpower to a global superpower able to strike CONUS targets with atomic warheads. While the United States had been able to use the power of the atomic bomb in its diplomacy against the Soviet Union since the last days of World War II, the advent of the Soviet bomb, combined with development of viable delivery systems beyond the obsolete Tu-4, while not introducing a climate of parity in nuclear strike capability with the United States, was seen as providing a viable deterrent to an American attack on the Soviet homeland. In the United States this deterrent was construed as a direct threat that had to be countered.

The lack of extensive accurate intelligence, misinterpretation of available intelligence and sometimes miss-direction by those vying for program funds, led to the United States unfounded fear that Soviet strategic bomber development in the early to late 1950's was more of a threat than it actually was. It was expected that by the early 1960's the Soviets could field a Mach 2.0 plus strategic bomber capable of operating at altitudes of 18593 m (~61,000 ft.) or greater. Such a bomber would be immune to interception by the Convair F-102 that had emerged as the winner of the MX-1554 competition to become the standard USAF ADC interceptor in the late 1950's. For the timeframe beyond 1962 the performance projections for the Soviet bomber threat was estimated at between Mach 2.2 to 2.7 at altitudes up to 19812 m (65,000 ft.). More or less in concert with the ongoing MX-1554 program, as early as 1953, United States research organisations were asked to look at the possibility of fielding an interceptor with cruise speeds up to Mach 4.05 in order to meet the projected post-1960's bomber threat. However, in the nearer term the MX-1554 proposal put forward by Republic – the AP-57 – held the promise of being able to counter low supersonic speed – up to Mach 2.0 – bombers expected to be fielded by the Soviet Union in the late 1950's or early 1960's.

As briefly noted above, at the time of the ADO release in January 1949, the Long-Range Aviation of the Soviet Union operated a fleet of Tu-4 'Bull', a reverse engineered version of the American Boeing B-29 Superfortress four piston engine long-range bomber. The Tu-4 had conducted its maiden flight in 1947 (Tupolev). With a maximum speed of 558 km/h (~347 mph) (Tupolev) the Tu-4 was vulnerable to interception even from the first generation of turbojet powered fighter aircraft just as the B-29 would prove to be inadequate against Soviet MiG-15 jet fighters during the Korean War, which entered ceasefire on 27 July 1953. With a maximum range of

6200 km (~3852.5 miles) the Tu-4 would, as noted above, have been adequate only for one way missions to be flown against contiguous CONUS targets.

Figure 1.2. In the late 1940's into the early 1950's the Soviet Union built a fleet of Tu-4 long-range bombers. Tupolev

Figure 1.3. The Myasishchev DBV-302 was an unbuilt long-range high altitude bomber concept proposed in 1946. Myasishchev

While the Tu-4 posed a threat in being to the United States, particularly once the Soviet Union had become an atomic armed power, the Soviet Union was developing more capable bombers as it sought to build up a nuclear strike capability to deter the United States from attacking the USSR. This bomber development effort took second place to efforts to field an ICBM (Intercontinental Ballistic Missile) force, which would guarantee a retaliatory strike against the United States following an American nuclear strike on the Soviet Union. The ICBM research would lead to the R-7A (8K71) (NATO reporting index SS-6), which conducted its first successful launch as an ICBM on August 1957 (it was an R-7 derivative that launched the world's first artificial Earth satellite – Sputnik-1 – at 22 hours 28 minutes and 34 seconds on 4 October 1957 (MODRF).

Figure 1.4. From the mid-1950's, the Soviet Union built-up of a fleet of Tu-95 turboprop powered intercontinental range bombers capable of attacking CONUS targets with nuclear weapons. Tupolev

There were a number of jet powered bomber programs being pursued by the Soviet Union in the late 1940's/early 1950's, including the Tupolev Tu-16, the prototype of which was flown on 27 April 1952. This was the first Soviet operational jet powered long range bomber. Production was authorised in December 1952, commenced in 1953 and ended in 1962 (MODRF & Tupolev). However, the Tu-16 lacked true intercontinental range – range was 7600 km (~4722 miles) – to provide a credible atomic deterrent able to strike contiguous CONUS targets if the Soviet homeland was attacked with atomic weapons. This capability was to be met with a much larger aircraft – the four Turboprop Tu-95 (allocated the NATO reporting name 'Bear'). The prototype Tu-95, '95/1', conducted its maiden flight on 12 November 1952 (Tupolev). Serial production of the first generation Tu-95 commenced in 1955 and the design entered Soviet service in 1957 – several hundred were manufactured in a plethora of variants – bomber, missile carrier, oceanic reconnaissance and special purpose (MODRF & Tupolev).

Figure 1.5. The Myasishchev M-4 (103M) and the later Myasishchev 3M (201M) (a 3M is shown in 1968) were developed as intercontinental range subsonic turbojet powered bombers capable of attacking CONUS targets with nuclear weapons. US DoD

The first Soviet turbojet powered intercontinental bomber was the Myasishchev M-4 (103M), the prototype of which conducted its maiden flight on 20 January 1953. Further development would lead to the 3M (201M), the prototype of which conducted its maiden flight on 27 March 1956 (Myasishchev). The 3M had a design maximum speed of 950 km/h (~580.30 mph), a ceiling of 11000 m (~36,089 ft.) and a design maximum range of 13000 km (~42,651 ft.). Neither of these bomber developments could attain supersonic speeds or the 15240 m (~50,000 ft.) plus altitudes that the XF-103 was intended to counter. However, the Soviets were working on a number of supersonic intercontinental range bomber developments, most notably the Myasishchev M-50 (allocated the NATO reporting name 'Bounder'). Designed as a strategic bomber/missile carrier, the M-50 was developed through to the flight test stage. In the strategic missile carrier role the M-50, which had a maximum design speed of 1950 km/h (~1,211.67 mph), a maximum operational ceiling of 16500 m (~54,134 ft.) and a 7400 km (~4598 mile) range. The bomber would have carried a large strategic strike air to surface missile designated B-3 (V-3). The 7400 km range would have been inadequate for deep strike missions against CONUS targets except on one way missions unless in-flight refueling was employed – this does not take into account any extended reach through the undisclosed range of the B-3 missile. The M-50 prototype conducted its maiden flight on 28 October 1959, the same year that the XF-103 program was terminated in its entirety (the program had been cancelled as a potential operational interceptor several years earlier). As performance was considered inadequate to ensure survival against the then perceived future air defence threat and the inadequate range for deep penetration CONUS strike missions, the M-50 program was cancelled in 1961– the last flight of this aircraft being conducted at the Tushino air parade on 9 July that year.

Figure 1.6. Soviet Myasishchev M-50 supersonic bomber flanked by two fighter aircraft.

The first generation of operational Soviet supersonic bombers was typified by the Tupolev Tu-22, the prototype of which, like the M-50, had conducted its maiden flight in 1959, the year the XF-103 program was terminated. This three crew design, powered by two VD-7 turbojet engines, had a maximum take-off weight of 92000 kg (~202,825 lb.), considerably in excess of the 54500 kg (~120,152 lb.) of the Tu-4 (Tupolev). Range of the Tu-22, at 5650 km (~3,511 miles), was inadequate for two way deep penetration CONUS missions, but could be employed on two way missions against targets in Alaska. The maximum speed of 1640 km/h (~1,019 mph) – ~Mach 1.34 – and a ceiling of 13500 m (~44,291 ft.) fell somewhat below that if the target set intended to be countered by the XF-103.

Figure 1.7. Unrealised Myasishchev M-30 concept of 1959 for a high-altitude nuclear (powered) aircraft that would have negated any range difficulties for deep penetration strikes on CONUS targets. Myasishchev

In the event, the threat (high supersonic speed high altitude – Mach 2 plus, 15240 m (50,000 ft. plus) Soviet bombers and the operational 18288-21336 m (~60,000-70,000 ft.) altitude capable Mach 3 defensive interceptors, intended to counter the bombers, did not materialise.

2

1954 AWI REPUBLIC MODEL AP-57 DESIGN ITERATION OF SEPTEMBER 1951 – PHASE 1 DEVELOPMENT

The design that would evolve into the Republic XF-103 was developed from the Republic AP-44A proposal dating back to early 1948. The AP-44A, which was designed as a high-speed, high altitude interceptor capable of operating in adverse weather conditions day and night, evolved into the AP-57, design of which was initiated in April 1950 (XF-103 CS, 1954). The AP-57 was one of the three Republic designs submitted to the USAF (United States Air Force) in January 1951 in response to a RFP (Request For Proposals) for the MX-1554. On 23 July 1951, the AP-57, along with single proposals from Lockheed and Convair (the latter being developed through to service variants as the F-102) were selected to proceed to the development phase – a Phase I development contract was awarded to Republic, this being amended in September 1951, for development of the AP-57 as the USAF Weapon System 204A.

From the issuing of the ADO (Advanced Development Objective) on 13 January 1949, it had been intended that the new interceptor would apply the new concept that was referred to as the weapon system concept. This envisioned the development of the airframe, engine, fire control system and even weapons, under a unified program rather than multiple programs in isolation – the weapon system concept was itself formulated in the period 1948-1949 (Knack, 1978). The fire control system selected for the MX-1554 was the Hughes MX-1179. This built on previous generation Hughes fire control systems commencing with the E-1 gunfire control radar installed in the Lockheed F-94A Starfire and the F-86A Sabre (Knack, 1978).

The 1954 AWI, Republic Model AP-57 was one of three pre-mock-up stage designs studied by Republic Aviation under the amended Phase I development contract awarded in September 1951. The primary mission was 'interception and destruction' of strategic bombers and air to surface missiles under clear/adverse weather conditions employing guided missiles and unguided rockets (WADC 1954 AWI, 1951). The primary mission envisioned operating under ground alert/control to counter 1955-1959 projected bomber threats (WADC 1954 AWI, 1951).

Figure 2.1. Partially ghosted artist rendering of the 1954 AWI Republic Model AP-57 in flight. This design was submitted to the USAF in January 1951. WADC

Documentation dated 10 September 1951 showed an aircraft design with a length of 73.6 ft. (~22.43 m); wingspan 35.7 ft. (~10.88 m); wing area 401 sq. ft. (~37.25 m^2); wing section, NACA 65A-003; height 18.7 ft. (~5.7 m); MAC, 179.4 ft. (~54.68 m) and tread, 11.2 ft. (~3.4 m). Projected weights for the design were 19,370 lb. (~8786 kg) empty (estimated); 20,470 lb. (~9285 kg) basic (estimated); 34,350 lb. (~15581 kg) design (estimated); 23,550 lb. (~10682 kg) for a point interception mission; 25,400 lb. (~11521 kg) for an area interception mission; 38,096 lb. (~17280 kg) maximum take-off weight – limited by structure strength – and 28,179 lb. (~12782 kg) maximum landing weight (WADC 1954 AWI, 1951).

DIMENSIONS

Wing
    Span: 35.7 ft. (~10.88 m)
    Incidence (variable): -4° to 14°
    Dihedral: 9°
    Sweepback (at leading-edge): 55°
Length: 73.6 ft. (~22.43 m)
Height: 18.7 ft. (~5.7 m)
Tread: 11.2 ft. (~3.4 m)

Table 2.1. Basic dimensions for the 1954 AWI Model AP-57 design iteration of 1951. WADC

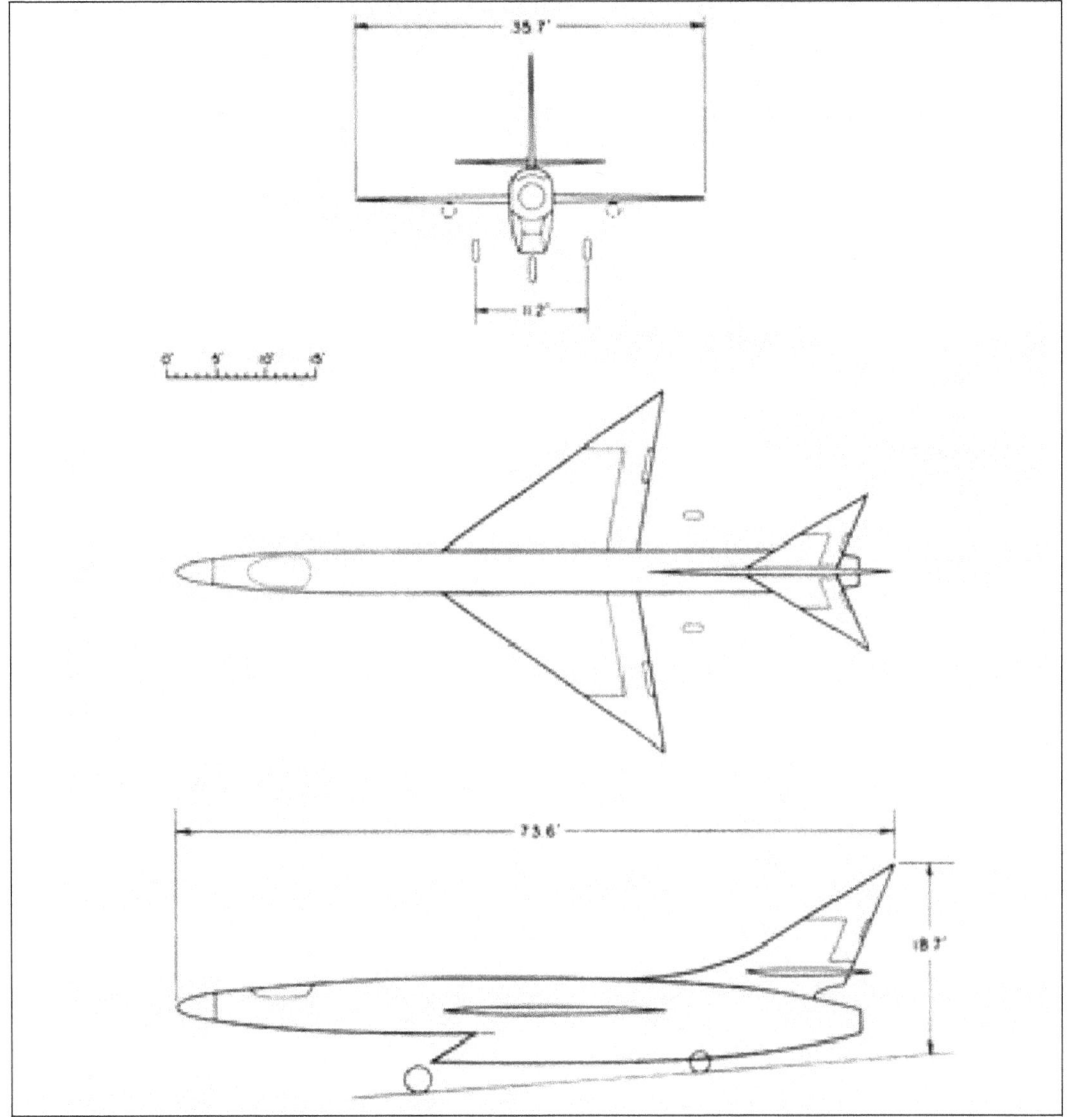

Figure 2.2. Three view general arrangement drawing of the 1954 AWI Republic Model AP-57 of 1951. WADC

The AP-57 design featured a variable incidence delta wing with 55° sweepback at the leading edge. The horizontal delta-tail, with a 60° leading-edge sweep, was more highly sweptback than the main delta wing. The design featured a tricycle undercarriage, which retracted to be accommodated in the fuselage. The landing run was to be reduced through employment of a brake parachute system. The pilot, electronic bay and cooling equipment were located in the forward fuselage section. The electronics suite would have included the Hughes Aircraft Corporation Integrated Electronics and Control System under the MX-1179. The pilot was seated in an escape capsule that formed an element of the adjustable pressurised cockpit, which would be retracted in flight. During take-off or landing the retractable cockpit would have been 'rotated up around a common hinge point', which would have allowed a better view over the aircraft nose section (WADC 1954 AWI, 1951).

1954 AWI REPUBLIC MODEL AP-57 OF 1951

WEIGHTS

Empty: 19,370 lb. (~8786 kg) – estimated
Basic: 20,470 lb. (~9285 kg) – estimated
Design: 34,350 lb. (~15581 kg)
Combat: 23,550 lb. (~10682 kg) – point interception
Combat: 25,400 lb. (~11521 kg) – area interception
Maximum take-off: 31,708 lb. (~14382.5 kg) – point interception
Maximum take-off: 38,096 lb. (~17280 kg) – area interception
Maximum landing: 28,179 lb. (~12782 kg)

Table 2.2. Basic dimensions of the 1954 AWI Republic Model AP-57 design iteration of 1951. WADC 1954 AWI, 1951

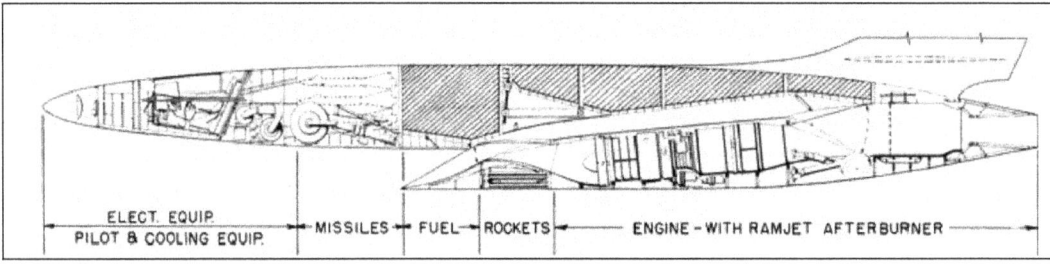

Figure 2.3. Port side-view ghosted graphic showing the various sections of the 1954 AWI Model AP-57 design iteration of 1951 – fore to aft: Electronic equipment; pilot & cooling group; missiles; rockets; engine with ramjet/afterburner. WADC

The aircraft was to be powered by a single Wright Aeronautical Corporation YJ67-W-1 (this designation is used in 1954 AWI Model AP-57 documentation dated 10 September 1951, but the YJ-67-W-3 designation was used from 1952 to reflect design modifications) axial flow turbojet. This engine, housed in the rear-central and rear fuselage sections, was designed to allow the afterburner section to be used independently as a ramjet combustion chamber using air by-passed around the turbo-jet engine compressor to increase available power when flying at speeds above Mach 2 (WADC 1954 AWI, 1951). At high Mach numbers the allowable turbine inlet temperature limited the engine thrust. Ramjet ratings were put at 30,000 lb. (~13607 kg) thrust at an altitude of 45,000 ft. (~13716 m) for a maximum speed of Mach 3.0 (WADC 1954 AWI, 1951). Air was to be fed to the engine through a Ferri style two-dimensional air intake, which formed the major element of the air inlet and transition section.

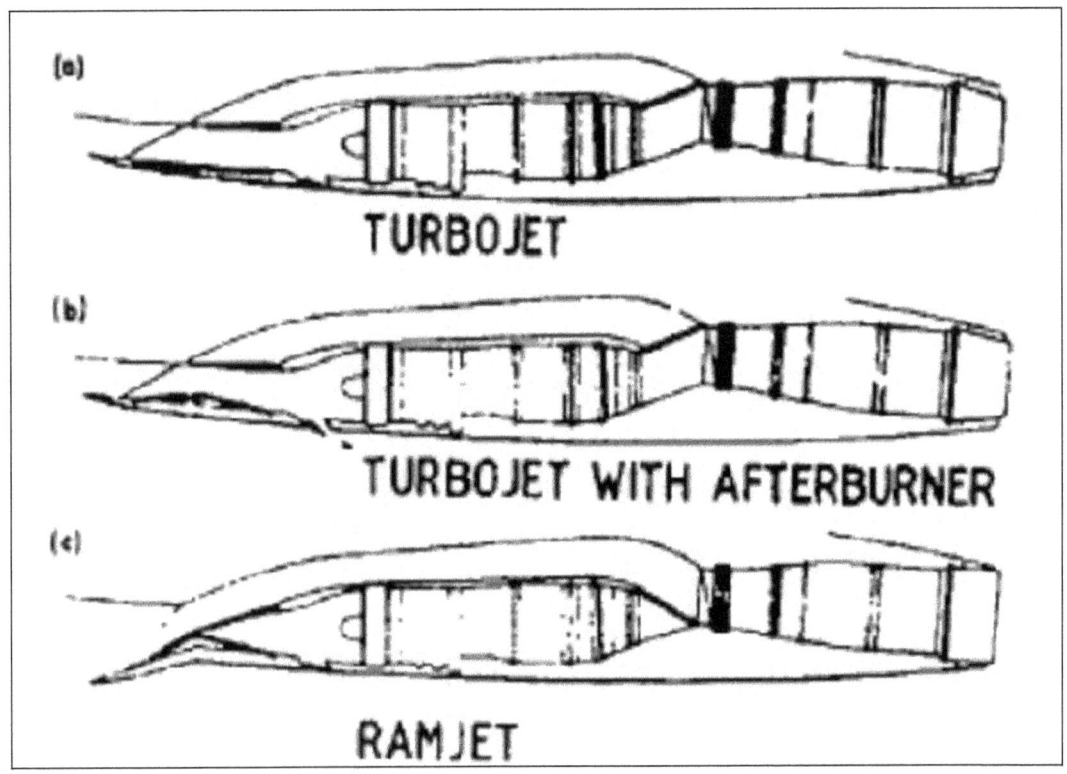

Figure 2.4. Graphic depicting the three operating modes of the Wright YJ67-W-1/3 power plant. (a). Operates as a turbojet engine on military power. (b). Operates on maximum turbojet power with the use of the afterburner section to increase thrust. (c). Operates as a ramjet whereby the afterburner section is employed independently as a ramjet combustion chamber using air by-passed around the turbojet engine compressor, increasing available power when flying at speeds above Mach 2. AGARD

Wright YJ67-W-1 power plant basic specification
Engine Spec No: AC-161A
Type: Axial
Length: 260.0 in. (~660.4 cm)
Diameter: 43.0 in. (~109.22 cm)
Weight (dry): 4,400 lb. (~1996 kg)
Tail pipe nozzle type: Two position
Tail pipe control type: Hydraulic
Augmentation: Afterburner (Afterburner is used independently as a ramjet when air is by-passed around the turbojet)

Table 2.3. Wright YJ67-W-1. WADC 1954 AWI, 1951

Wright YJ67-W-1 engine ratings			
S.L. Static	Thrust	RPM	Minutes
Maximum	19,600 lb. (~8890 kg) – with afterburner	6600	5
Military	11800 lb. (~5352 kg)	6600	30
Normal	9700 lb. (~4409 kg)	6600	Continuously

Table 2.4. Wright YJ67-W-1 engine ratings. WADC 1954 AWI, 1951

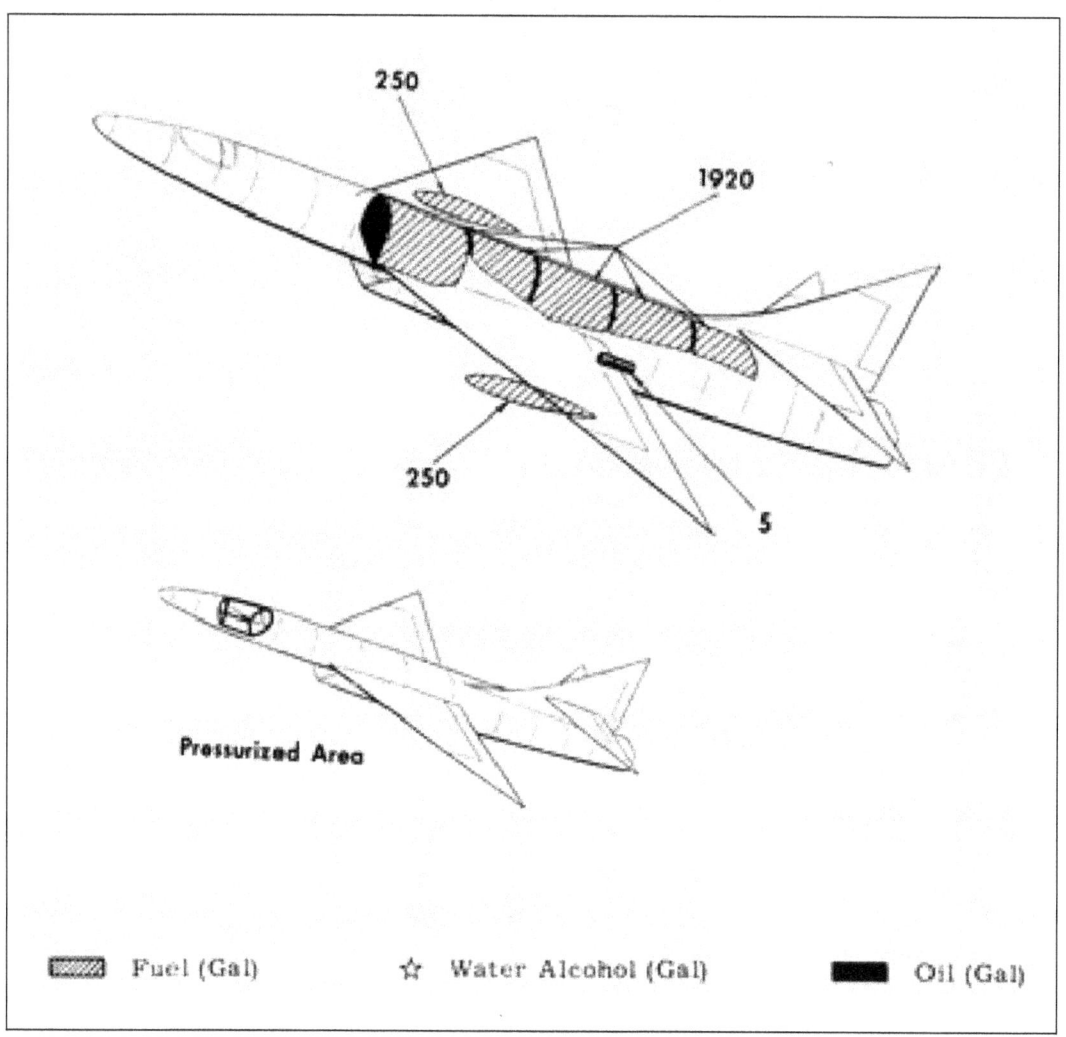

Figure 2.5. Graphic showing the pilots pressurised compartment in the forward fuselage section and the JP-3 Grade fuel and 1010 Grade oil tankage amounting to 2420 gal and 5 gal respectively. WADC/Republic Archives

The maximum internal fuel capacity was set at 1920 gal of JP-3 Grade housed in five fuselage fuel tanks – these lacked self-sealing or armour protection. Two external fuel tanks could be carried – one on each wing – each holding 250 gal., giving a combined internal and external fuel capacity of 2420 gal of JP-3 fuel. The aircraft had capacity for 5 gal of 1010 Grade oil. Ground refueling was single-point. The design featured a 'continuous fuel purging system' – for internal and external fuel tanks – which would maintain both external and internal purging of the aircraft fuel cells (WADC 1954 AWI, 1951).

The aircraft design was to be armed with six XAAM-2-A (Experimental Air to Air Missile-2-A) (MX-904) Falcon guided air to air missiles and a battery of 36 x 2.75 in. (~6.985 cm) unguided FFAR (Folding Fin Aircraft Rockets), all of which would have been carried internally. The XAAM-2-A missiles would have been housed in racks within an internal weapon bay accessed through the aircraft central-forward fuselage underside, aft of the cockpit area. Three missiles would have been located on each side on short zero launch rails. During the missile launch sequence the weapon bay doors would be opened and the missile racks extended, the missile then launching. The FFAR's were housed on doors that were located around the air duct for the YJ67-W-1 engine, a potential problem source (WADC 1954 AWI, 1951).

The aircraft would have required a non-assisted ground run of 3,150 ft. (~960 m) and 4,600 ft. (~1402 m) to reach an altitude of 50 ft. (~15.24 m) – values for an area interception mission. Maximum speed at sea level was 782 knots (~1448 km/h) at maximum turbojet power and combat speed increased to 1724 knots (~3193 km/h) at maximum ramjet power and at an altitude of 60,000 ft. (~18288 m). At a point interception mission take-off weight of 31,708 lb. (~14383.5 kg) the aircraft was to be capable of take-off, accelerating and climb to 40,000 ft. (~12192 m) on maximum turbojet power and then further accelerating and climbing to 60,000 ft. (~18288 m) at maximum ramjet power in a time of 9.54 minutes. At point interception take-off weight the aircraft was to have a seal level climb rate of 23,400 fpm – feet per minute (~7132 m/pm – metres per minute) at maximum turbojet power, increasing to 35,000 fpm (~10668 m/pm) at 60,000 ft. (~18288 m) at maximum ramjet power. Ceiling was put at 28,500 ft. (~8686.8 m) at 100 fpm (~30.48 m/pm) and normal power at a point interception take-off weight. Ceiling at 500 fpm (~152.4 m/pm), maximum turbojet power and combat weight (not stated as point or area intercept) was put at 56,500 ft. (~17221 m) (WADC 1954 AWI, 1951). No values were provided for stalling speed. Combat range was put at 1716 nm (~3179 km) when loaded with a 1,291 lb. (~586 kg) payload at an average speed of 474 knots (~878 km/h) in a mission time of 3.56 hours (no weight values were given – point or area intercept) (WADC 1954 AWI, 1951).

Mission scenario I – Point interception. The 1951 AP-57 iteration was to be capable of taking off and, under maximum power, climbing to an altitude of 40,000 ft. (~12192 m). The aircraft would then accelerate to a speed of 1150 knots (Mach 2.0) while remaining at 40,000 ft. altitude. The aircraft would then employ ramjet power to accelerate to 1724 knots (Mach 3.0) and then climb to an altitude of 60,000 ft. (~18288 m), still under ramjet power, before releasing weapons with an allowance of 5 minutes for the combat phase, still under ramjet power. The aircraft would then decelerate to the most economical cruise speed to achieve maximum endurance, reducing altitude to 30,000 ft. (~9144 m) for a 15 minute loiter. Additional mission time allowances included a 30 second period at military power setting and a further 5 minutes at 50% RPM (Revolutions Per Minute) for ground operations – engine start and ground taxi for take-off – with a fuel reserve allowance to enable a 10 minute loiter at sea level and acceleration from landing speed to double landing speed. Collective phases of the point interception would total a time of 29.53 minutes (WADC 1954 AWI, 1951).

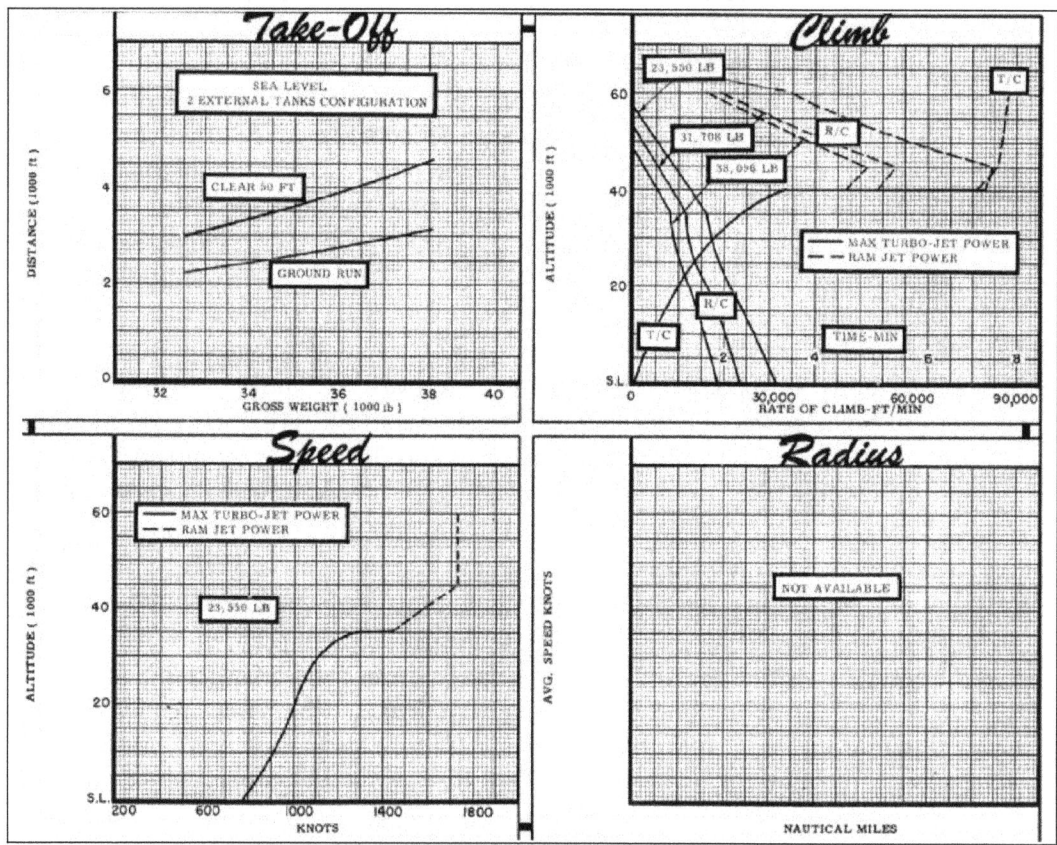

Figure 2.6. Quartet of graphs showing the various performance traits of the AWI Model AP-57 iteration of 1951, based on contractor data for take-off, climb, speed and radius performance (this latter category is bereft of data). WADC

Mission scenario II – Radius. The 1951 AP-57 design iteration was to be capable of taking off and, under maximum power, climbing to an altitude of 40,000 feet (~12192 m). The aircraft would then jettison external fuel tanks before accelerating, under ramjet power, to a speed of 1150 knots (Mach 2.0) whilst remaining at 40,000 ft. (~12192 m) altitude. The aircraft would then accelerate to 1438 knots (Mach 2.5) and climb to an altitude of 60,000 ft. (~18288 m), still under ramjet power, before releasing weapons with an allowance of 3 minutes for the combat phase. The aircraft would then decelerate to the most economical cruise speed to achieve maximum endurance, reducing altitude to that considered most economical, with a 15 minute loiter in the combat area at 30,000 ft. (~9144 m). Additional mission time allowances included a 30 second period at military power setting and a further 5 minutes at 50% RPM for ground operations – engine start and ground taxi for take-off – with a fuel reserve allowance to enable a 10 minute loiter at sea level, acceleration from landing speed to double landing speed and the 3 minute combat phase noted above. A typical area intercept mission was estimated to cover an area of 275 nm (~509 km) at an average speed of 692 knots (~1281.5 km/h) for a mission duration of 1.38 hours (WADC 1954 AWI, 1951).

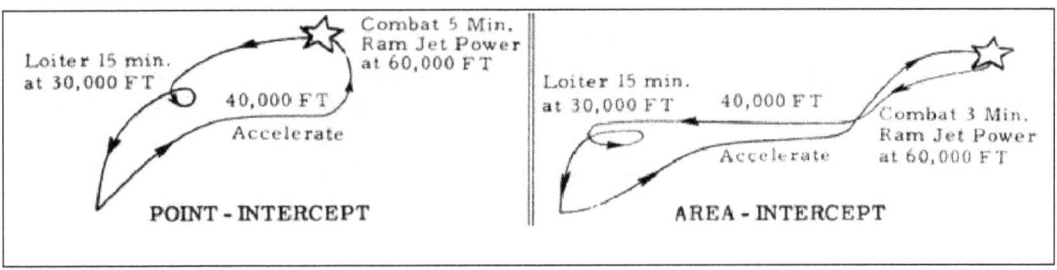

Figure 2.7. Graphics showing the basic profile for the two main missions envisioned for the AWI Republic Model AP-57 of 1951 – Point intercept and Area intercept. WADC

On Mission scenario III the 1951 AP-57 design iteration was to be capable of taking off under maximum power and climbing to an undetermined altitude (probably 30,000 ft. (~9144 m) for cruise flight at the most economical long-range speed – external fuel tanks would be jettisoned once the fuel contained in them had been consumed. The aircraft would loiter for 15 minutes at economical cruise speed and 30,000 ft. altitude at undetermined range before returning to base. Additional mission time allowances included a 30 second period at military power setting and a further 5 minutes at 50% RPM for ground operations – engine start and ground taxi for take-off – 15 minute loiter, noted above, and an additional ten minutes loiter at sea level with a fuel reserve for acceleration from landing speed to double landing speed (WADC 1954 AWI, 1951).

Following design approval in September 1951, the AP-57 program moved to the mock-up stage conducted in March 1953, with a projected prototype first flight scheduled for February 1957. All performance data employed in relation to the AWI Republic Model AP-57 of 1951 was that calculated by the contractor – Republic Aviation – and was not substantiated by Wright Air Development Centre at the time of the documentation release in September 1951. The performance data for the Wright Aeronautical YJ67-W-1 double (dual)-cycle power plant was that provided by Wright Aeronautics – performance specification for both the aircraft design and the power plant would be subjected to a number of changes post-mock-up review.

1954 AWI Model AP-57 of 1951 loading and performance characteristics (WADC, based on contractor data)

Loading and Performance – Typical Missions

Conditions	Point intercept	Area intercept	Ferry Range
Take-off weight	31,708 lb.	38.096 lb.	38.096 lb.
Fuel at 6.5 lb./gal (JP-3)	9,729 lb.	15,617 lb.	15,617 lb.
Load (rockets & missiles)	1,291 lb.	1,291 lb.	1,291 lb.
Wing loading	79 lb./ft.^{2}	95 lb./ft.^{2}	95 lb./ft.^{2}
Take-off run, sea level		3,160 ft.	3,160 ft.
Take-off to clear 50 ft.	3,000 ft.	4,600 ft.	4,600 ft.
Rate of climb, sea level	23,400 fpm	18,600 fpm	4,150 fpm
Climb from sea level-40,000 ft.	4.45 minutes	6.3 minutes	10.4 minutes
Climb from sea level-60,000 ft.	9.53 minutes	19.8 minutes	
Ceiling (100 fpm)	51,500 ft.	40,250 ft.	26,200 ft.
Combat range		1716 nm	1716 nm
Average speed		474 knots	474 knots
Initial cruising altitude		25,000 ft.	25,000 ft.
Final cruise altitude		35,000 ft.	35,000 ft.
Total mission time		3.56 hours	3.56 hours
Combat radius		375 nm	
Average speed		682 knots	
Initial cruise altitude		60,000 ft.	
Interception altitude	60,000 ft.	60,000 ft.	
Final cruise altitude		40,000 ft.	
Total mission time	0.492 hours	1.38 hours	
Combat weight (average)	23,550 lb.	25,400 lb.	22,021 lb.
Combat altitude	60,000 ft.	60,000 ft.	35,000 ft.
Combat speed	1724 knots	1724 knots	1290 knots
Combat climb	35,000 fpm	30,000 fpm	17,000 fpm
Combat ceiling (500 fpm)	56,500 ft.		57,500 ft.
Combat ceiling (100 fpm)	57,000 ft.		58,000 ft.
Maximum climb rate, sea level	31,000 fpm	29,200 fpm	32,600 fpm
Maximum speed at sea level	782 knots	780 knots	783 knots
Landing weight	20,688 lb.	20,688 lb.	20,688 lb.
Landing distance from 50 ft.	2,940 ft.	2,940 ft.	2,940 ft.

Table 2.5. Loading and performance calculations for the AP-57 design iteration of 1951 – typical missions. Note: There are two initial and final cruise altitude lines under 'Conditions', with values provided for each. Documentation is confusing, but the first value for each appears to be for a ferry range mission whilst the second value for each is for an interception mission, regardless of layout. WADC 1954 AWI, 1951

3

XF-103 (AP-57) DESIGN ITERATION OF JANUARY 1954

Following a successful full-scale mock-up inspection in March 1953 it was intended that the Republic AP-57 submitted to the MX-1554 program office would proceed to Phase II development. However, the Phase II contract was suspended and the Phase I contract was extended for a period of 18 months beyond the mock-up inspection (Knack, 1978). During the extended Phase I contract period a number of redesigns were thrashed out through a series of tests, including wind-tunnel tests, interception of bomber aircraft flying at speeds up to Mach 1.3 remaining the primary mission of the resultant Republic MX-1554 design iteration of 1954 (NACA RM SL54H2, 1954). The most outwardly visible of the changes incorporated in the 1954 design iteration, now officially designated XF-103, was the rearrangement of the tail-plane units, which were lowered from the upper rear fuselage at the base of the vertical tail of the 1951 AP-57 to the lower rear fuselage on the 1954 XF-103. Other outward changes included a reinforcement of the flush canopy concept and incorporation of a periscope system to afford the pilot a forward view of the outside world to compensate for removal of the upper/forward view canopy (SAC XF-103, 1954). The 18 month extension to the Phase I contract was provisioned in order to allow time for the development of technology required to implement the changes proposed at the mock-up review – the periscope system for instance (Knack, 1978) and other refinements through a process of tunnel testing.

During 1953, a series of wind-tunnel tests were conducted to prove the design, including tests conducted on a 1/15-scale model at speeds of Mach 1.45 and Mach 1.9, and tests with a 1/10-scale model to measure the low-speed stability and control characteristics of the revised Republic MX-1554 (XF-103) (NACA RM SL54H2, 1954). Wind-tunnel tests were also conducted on a 1/60-scale model of Republic's revised MX-1554 (XF-103) in order to investigate the designs 'static longitudinal and lateral stability and the control characteristics' (NACA SA53C18, 1953). The tests were conducted at Mach 2.85 and Reynolds number 2.45×10^6, determined from the 'mean aerodynamic chord of the wing' (NACA SA53C18, 1953).

Figure 3.1. Post-mock-up inspection the Republic AP-57 was redesigned to incorporate a number of changes, including lowering of the tail-planes and reinforcing the flush canopy concept with a periscope observation system. NMUSAF

In 1953, tests on a 1/30-scale model were conducted to determine the stability and control characteristics of the revised Republic MX-1554A design at high subsonic speeds. The tests were conducted in the Langley 7 ft. by 10 ft. (2.13 m by 3.04 m) wind-tunnel at speeds ranging from Mach 0.40 to 0.95 (NACA RM SL53K12a, 1953). These tunnel tests built on the low speed tunnel test phase that was conducted on a 1/10-scale model (NACA RM SL53A05, 1953).

Wind-tunnel testing continued beyond the issue date of the XF-103 data that is the main subject of this chapter. This included August 1954 tunnel tests of an XF-103 1/30-scale model that were conducted in the NASA Langley transonic tunnel in order to determine the 'longitudinal stability and control characteristics' of the design, as well as 'the effect of speed brakes located at the end of the fuselage (NACA RM SL54H2, 1954). The majority of these tests were conducted with 'internal flow', but some research data was obtained with the model in non-internal flow (NACA RM SL54H2, 1954). Through data obtained with the transonic speed tests, at Reynolds numbers of 1.8×10^6, no 'serious longitudinal stability and control problems' were found (NACA RM SL54H2, 1954). Transonic drag rise was found to be modest and the speed brakes produced no noticeable 'adverse effects on longitudinal stability' of the design (NACA RM SL54H2, 1954).

Figure 3.2. A 1/30-scale model of the Republic MX-1554A (XF-103), fitted with wing fences and 55° speed brakes, in the NACA Langley 7ft. by 10 ft. wind-tunnel. NASA (NACA RM SL54H24)

Figure 3.3. 1/30-scale model of the Republic MX-1554A (XF-103) during stability and control characteristic tests at high subsonic speeds in the NACA Langley 7 ft. by 10 ft. wind-tunnel. NASA (NACA RM SL53K12a)

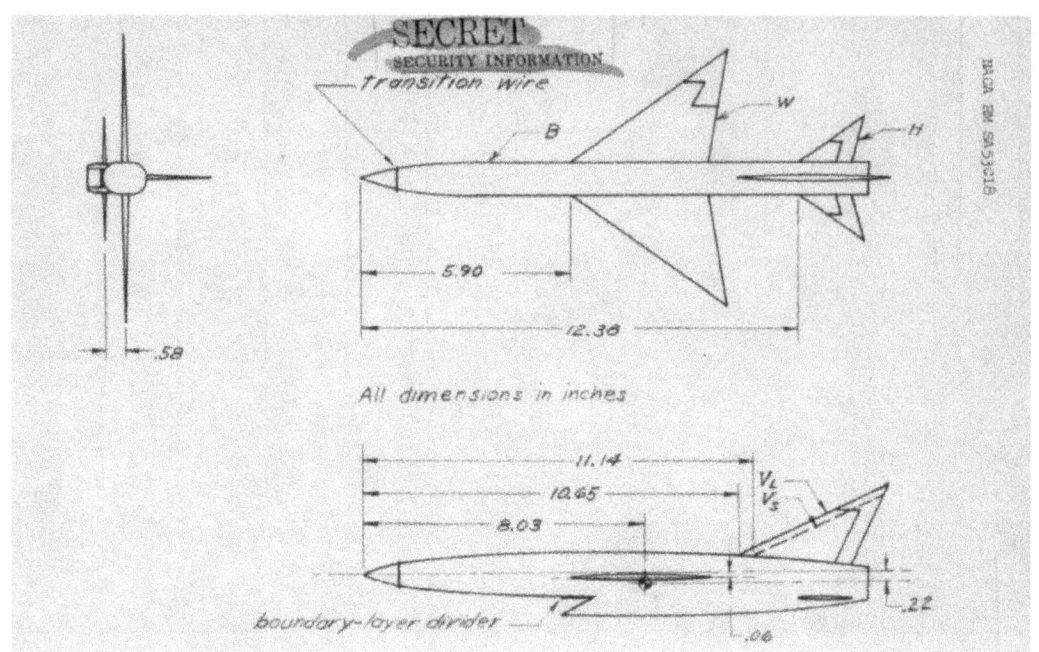

Figure 3.4. Three-view general arrangement drawing of the 1/60-scale model of the Republic MX-1554 (XF-103). NASA (NACA RM SA53C18)

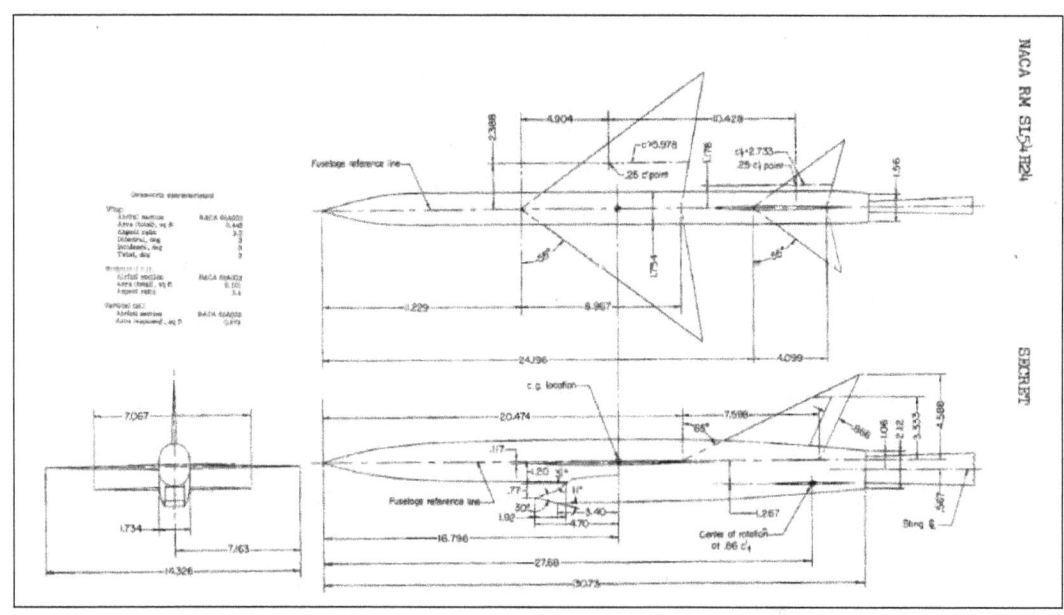

Figure 3.5. Three-view general arrangement drawing of a 1/22-scale model of the XF-103 tested in the NACA Langley 8 ft. transonic wind-tunnel (Dimensions are given in inches except where noted). NASA (NACA RM SL54H24)

In June 1954, Republic Aviation was awarded a contract for the construction of three post mock-up review redesign XF-103 (AP-57) development aircraft (Knack, 1978). In documentation dated January 1954, a first flight was estimated for February 1957 (CS XF-103, 1954). The Phase II development contract for the Weapons System 204A (XF-103) was awarded to Republic in September 1954 (Knack, 1978). By this time it was clear that the Convair F-102 was progressing toward service as the USAF (United States Air Force) MX-1554 interceptor. The XF-103, if not yet by official decree, then by default, had effectively taken on the role of research and development into technologies for possible future application on a service interceptor.

When the post-mock-up stage XF-103 characteristics document was presented on 5 January 1954, the primary mission was detailed as 'the interception and destruction of hostile aircraft under all conditions of weather and visibility', there being no mention of the missile target set laid down in the September 1951 AP-57 iteration (SAC XF-103, 1954). The document went on to state that the design was intended to fulfill the missions of local and general air defence (SAC XF-103, 1954). The 1954 XF-103 (AP-57) design was still identifiable with the 1951 AP-57, retaining the delta-wing (NACA 65A-003) and tail-plane layout and polished fuselage with a flush cockpit (redesigned, as noted above). The fuselage design was of 'rectangular cross-sections in the region adjacent to the fuselage base' (NACA RM SL54H24, 1954). A feature not mentioned in 1951 AP-57 documentation was the 'hydraulic power-operated irreversible surface controls' (SAC XF-103, 1954). Major control surfaces included the double-slotted wing flaps, speed brakes and the 'adjustable air-scoop' for the turbojet/ramjet engine with the nozzle at the extreme rear of the fuselage (SAC XF-103, 1954). The under-fuselage supersonic scoop inlet was of rectangular shape and featured side walls that were sweptback (NACA RM SL54H24, 1954). The aircraft would operate under turbojet power from zero-airspeed to Mach 2.1 when the switch would be made to ramjet power through the by-passing of the turbojet (SAC XF-103, 1954).

Design documentation showed an aircraft with a length of 76.8 ft. (~23.4 m) (an increase of 3.2 ft. (0.97 m) over that of the 1951 AP-57); wingspan 34.4 ft. (~10.48 m) (a reduction of 1.3 ft. (~0.4 m) over that of the 1951 AP-57); height 16.5 ft. (~5 m) (a reduction of 3.2 ft. (~0-97 m) from the 1951 AP-57); tread 11.3 ft. (~3.44 m) (an increase of 0.1 ft. over that of the 1951 AP-57). As noted above, the NACA 65A-003 wing section was retained from the 1951 AP-57 design. Wing area, at 401 sq. ft. (~37.25 m^2), remained the same as for the 1951 AP-57. Aspect ratio was 3.2; height 18.7 ft. (~5.7 m); MAC, 179.4 ft. (~54.68 m) – a 0.07 ft. reduction from the 1951 AP-57) (SAC XF-103, 1954).

Projected weights were 24,959 lb. (~11321 kg) empty (an increase of 5,579 lb. (~2531 kg) over that of the 1951 AP-57); 31,219 lb. (~14161 kg) for a point interception mission (an increase of 7,669 lb. (~3479 kg) over that of the 1951 AP-57); 33,764 lb. (~15315 kg) for an area interception mission (an increase of 8,364 lb. (~3794 kg) over that of the 1951 AP-57); 38,505 lb. (~17466 kg) maximum take-off for a point interception mission and 42,864 lb. (~19896 kg) maximum take-off for an area interception mission (CS XF-103, 1954).

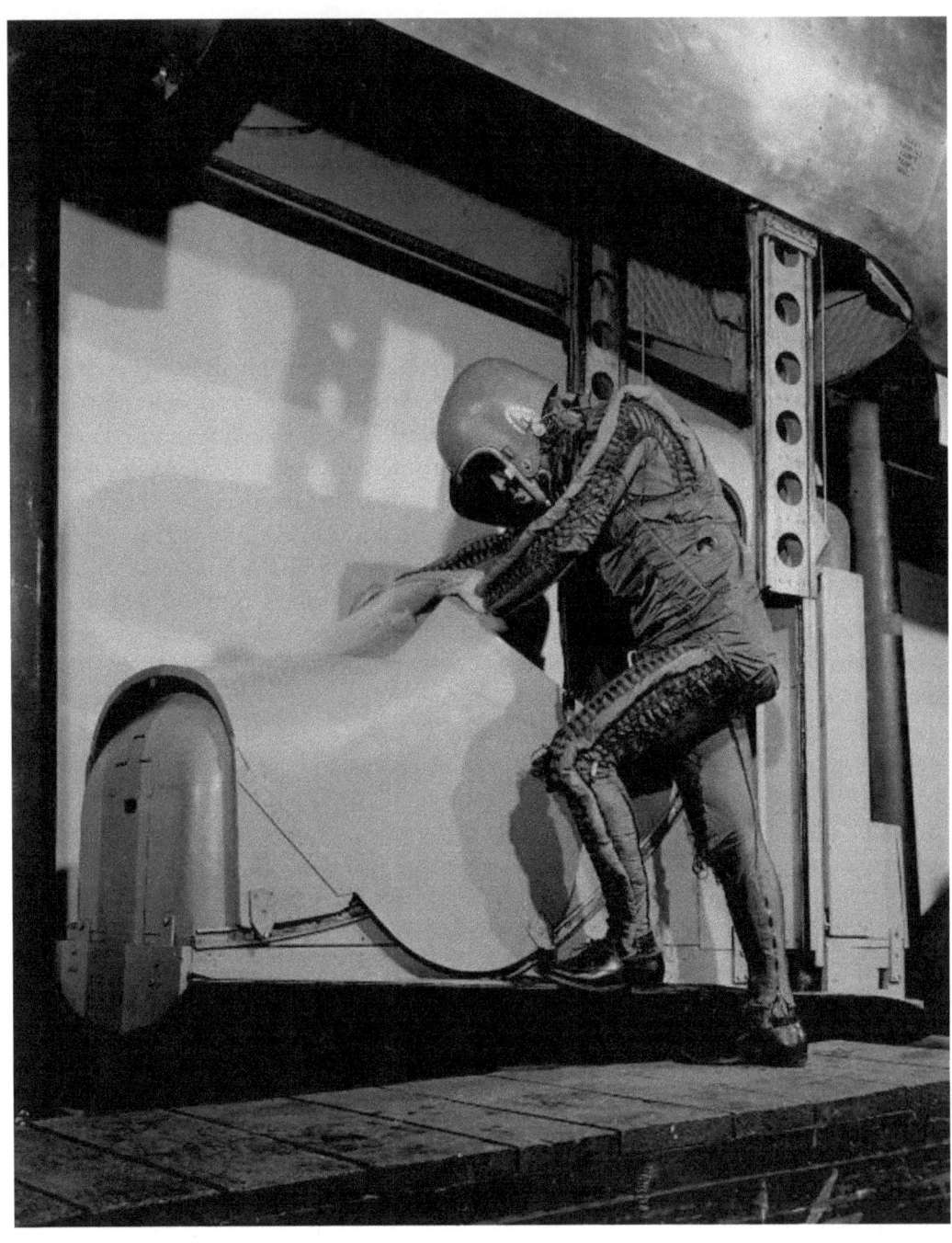

Figure 3.6. Mock-up of the escape capsule for the Republic XF-103 (AP-57) pilot with a manikin adorned with a high-altitude pressure suit. NMUSAF

The aircraft structure was manufactured primarily of titanium. The electronics bay was located in the nose section, aft of which was the air conditioned cockpit section incorporating a single-crew capsule for the pilot whom was adorned with a pressure flight suit. The two weapon bays were located aft of the cockpit section, this arrangement being distinct from the arrangement incorporated in the 1954 AP-57 design iteration of September 1951. The air inlet and transition section was located aft of the missile bays with the turbojet engine housed in the central-rear fuselage section with the rear undercarriage aft of the turbojet and the afterburner/ramjet section in the rear fuselage, exiting through the tail (SAC XF-103, 1954).

The primary detection and targeting sensor remained the Hughes Aircraft Company MX-1179 Integrated Electronics and Control System, which was designed to meet the mission requirement for automatic execution of the target interception process, including launching of missile and rocket armament. The MX-1179 also handled flight navigation and communication functions (SAC XF-103, 1954).

The double (dual)-cycle power plant intended for the 1954 AP-57 design iteration of September 1951 was retained in the XF-103 (AP-57) of 1954, but the axial flow turbojet now carried the designation YJ67-W-3. When air was by-passed the independent afterburner section functioned as the XRJ55-W-1 ramjet. The basic specification and performance characteristics of the combined YJ67-W-3/ XRJ55-W-1 changed in a number of areas, see Tables 3.3 & 3.4. Fuel capacity was increased from 2420 to 2440 gal; fueling being accomplished through a single point refueling system.

Figure 3.7. Artist rendering of the MX-1554A Republic AP-57 design iteration of 1954, by which time it was known as the XF-103. The ghosted forward section shows, from fore to aft, the Hughes Electronic Control System, the pressurised pilot compartment and the weapon bays housing six XGAR-1 semi-active radar guided air to air missiles. SAC XF-103, 1954/Republic Archives

DIMENSIONS
Wing
    Span: 34.4 ft. (~10.48 m)
    Incidence (root): 0°
    Incidence (tip): 0°
    Dihedral: 0°
    Sweepback (leading edge): 55°
Length: 76.8 ft. (~23.40 m)
Height: 16.6 ft. (~5.0 m)
Tread: 11.3 ft. (~3.44 m)

Table 3.1. Basic dimensions of the MX-1554A Republic XF-103 (AP-57) design iteration of 1954. SAC XF-103, 1954

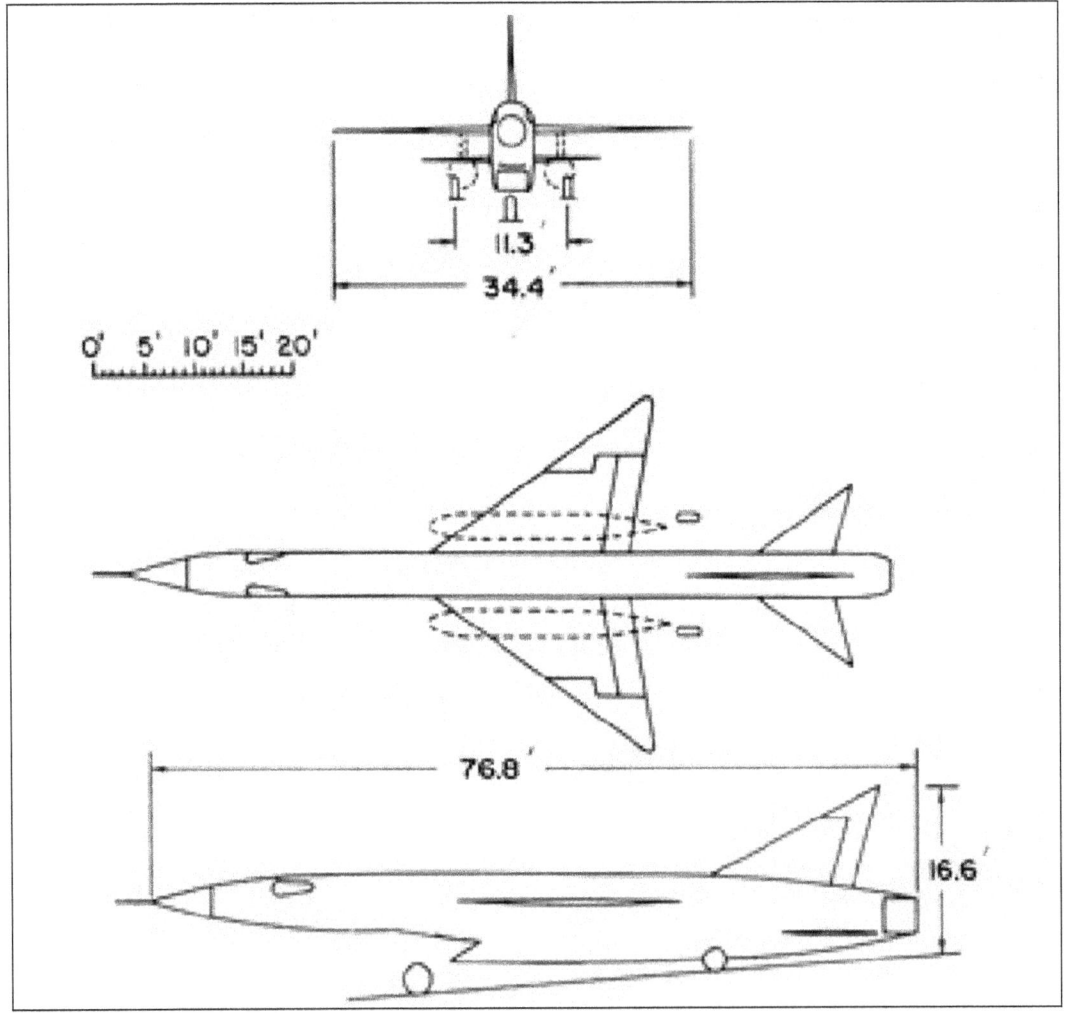

Figure 3.8. Three view general arrangement drawing of the MX-1554A Republic XF-103 (AP-57) design iteration of 1954. SAC XF-103, 1954

WEIGHTS

Empty (calculated): 24,959 lb. (~11321 kg)
Basic (calculated): 25,259 lb. (~11457 kg)
Design: 32,000 lb. (~14515 kg)
Combat (point intercept): 31,219 lb. (~14161 kg)
Combat (area intercept): 33,764 lb. (~15315 kg)
Maximum take-off (area intercept): 42,864 lb. (~19896 kg), limited by performance
Maximum landing: 34,300 lb. (~15558 kg), limited by strength

Table 3.2. Basic projected weights of the MX-1554A Republic XF-103 (AP-57) design iteration of 1954. SAC XF-103, 1954

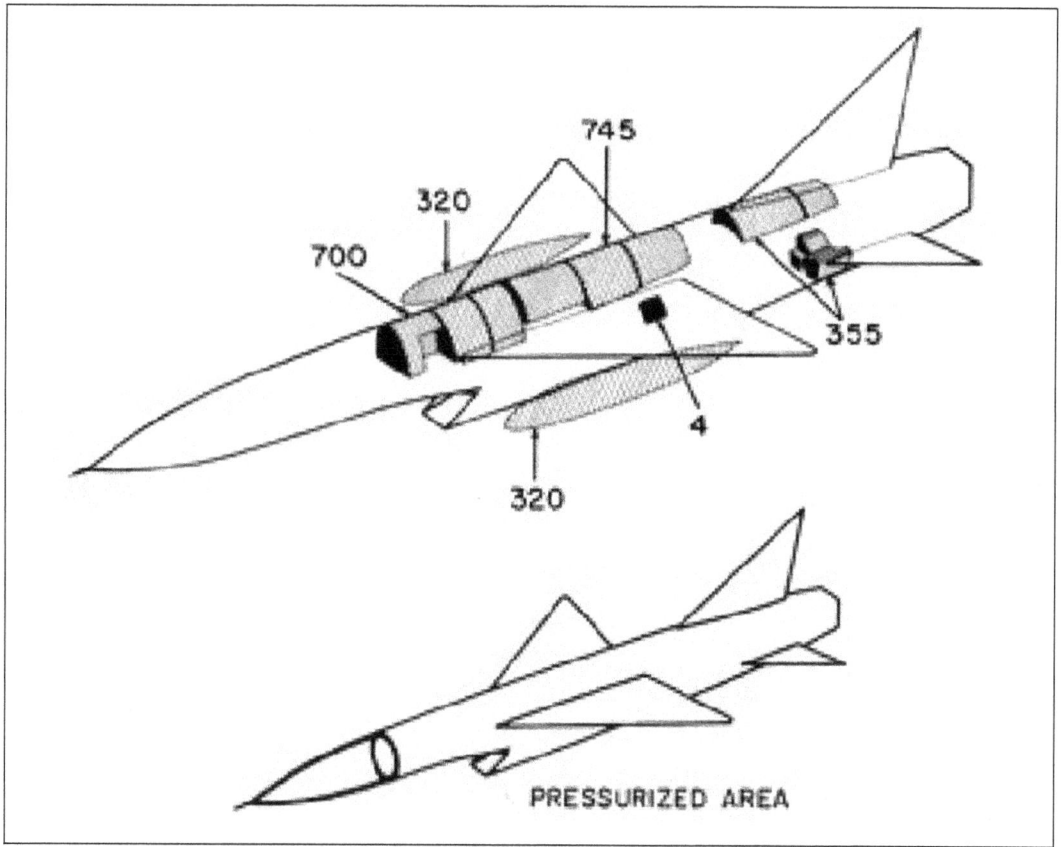

Figure 3.9. Graphic showing the pilot pressurised compartment in the forward fuselage section and the JP-4 Grade fuel and 1010 Grade oil tankage, amounting to 2440 gal and 4 gal respectively, of the MX-1554A Republic XF-103 (AP-57) design iteration of 1954. SAC XF-103, 1954

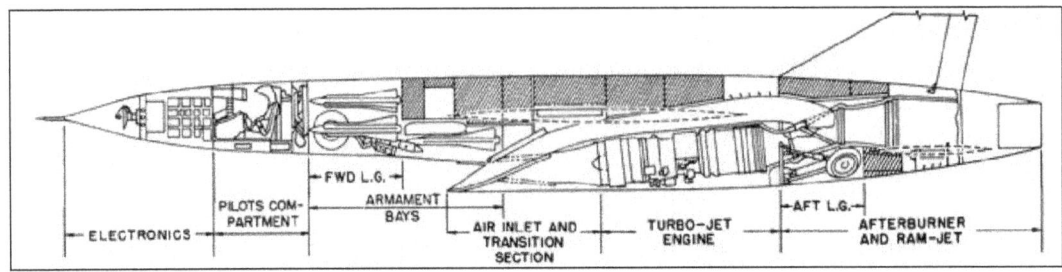

Figure 3.10. Port side-view ghosted graphic of various sections of the MX-1554A XF-103 (AP-57) design iteration of 1954, showing fore to aft: electronic equipment, pilot compartment, forward undercarriage unit, armament bays, air inlet and transition section, engine, afterburner/ramjet and aft undercarriage. SAC XF-103, 1954

As well as a marginal increase in fuel capability under specification MIL-F-5624A, the distribution of fuel tankage was completely redesigned. Now 700 gal was carried in 3 forward fuselage tanks, 745 gal. was carried in 3 main fuselage tanks, 355 gal was housed in 5 aft fuselage tanks and 640 gal could be carried in two jettisonable external wing tanks for a combined total of 2440 gal. JP-4 Grade fuel – the AP-57 iteration of 1951 burned JP-3 fuel (CS XF-103, 1954). Oil tankage was reduced from 5 gal in the 1954 AWI Model AP-57 of 1951 to 4 gal 1010 Grade oil under specification MIL-L-6081A, housed in a single tank in the fuselage (SAC XF-103, 1954).

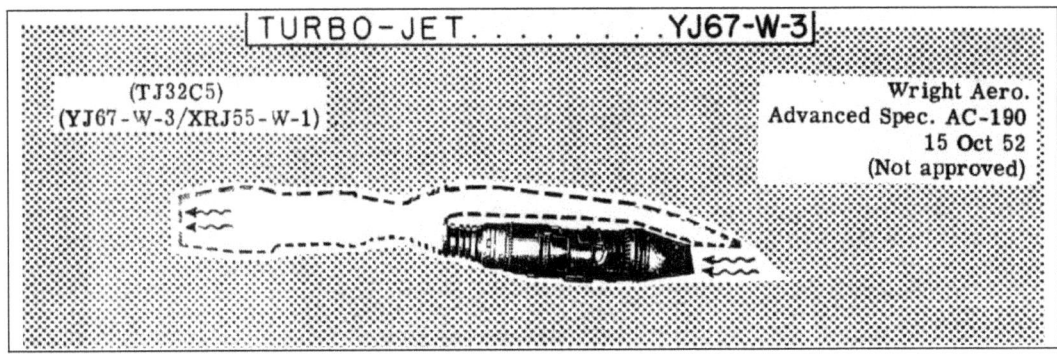

Figure 3.11. Basic layout diagram of the YJ67-W-3/XRJ55-W-1 double (dual) cycle engine intended for the XF-103. AECS YJ67-W-3, 1953

The YJ67-W-3 compressors were of the axial, twin spool type – one low pressure, 5-stage and one high pressure, 7-stage. Maximum design pressure ratio/SLS was 10.5:1. Two axial single-stage turbines would drive the low and high pressure compressors. The combustion was annular with fuel nozzles and a variable area exhaust nozzle. Maximum rated through turbine inlet temperature was 1600° Fahrenheit (AECS YJ67-W-3, 1953). The YJ67-W-3 was designed with an operating altitude up to 65,000 ft. (~19812 m) and an absolute altitude of 75,000 ft. (~22860 m), with a maximum starting altitude of 35,000 ft. (~10668 m) (AECS YJ67-W-3, 1953).

> Wright YJ67-W-3/XRJ55-W-1 double (dual)-cycle power plant – afterburner operates as a ramjet
>
> No: 1
> Engine Spec No: AC-190
> Type: Double-Cycle, Axial
> Length: 534.0 in. (~1356.36 cm)
> Diameter: 52.0 in. (~132.08 cm)
> Weight (dry): 6,904 lb. (~3131.6 kg) – includes the ramjet and accessories
> Tail pipe nozzle type: Variable Area
> Tail pipe control type: Hydraulic
> Augmentation: Afterburner. Afterburner is used independently as a ramjet when air is by-passed around the turbojet

Table 3.3. Wright YJ67-W-3/XRJ55-W-1 double (dual)-cycle power plant basic specification for the XF-103 design iteration of 1954. CS XF-103, 1954/SAC XF-103, 1954

> Wright YJ67-W-3/XRJ55-W-1 double (dual)-cycle power plant – afterburner operates as a ramjet
>
> Turbojet ratings
>
> | S.L. Static | Thrust, lb. | RPM | SCF (lb./lb./hr.) | Time, minutes |
> |---|---|---|---|---|
> | Maximum | 22,350 (afterburner*) | 6175 | 2,350 (WAB) | 5 |
> | Military | 12,950 | 6175 | 0.795 | 30 |
> | Normal | 11,400 | 6175 | Cont. | |
> | 90% norm thrust | 10,260 | 6175 | | |
> | 75% norm thrust | 8,550 | 5920 | | |
> | Idle | ------ (max) | 2500 | | |
>
> * Utilises the ramjet function
>
> Ramjet ratings
>
> Design Mach number: 3.0
> Altitude: 55,000 ft. (~16764 m)
> Thrust 18,800 lb. (~8537.3 kg)

Table 3.4. Wright YJ67-W-3/XRJ55-W-1 double (dual)-cycle power plant ratings for the XF-103 design iteration of 1954. CS XF-103, 1954/SAC XF-103, 1954

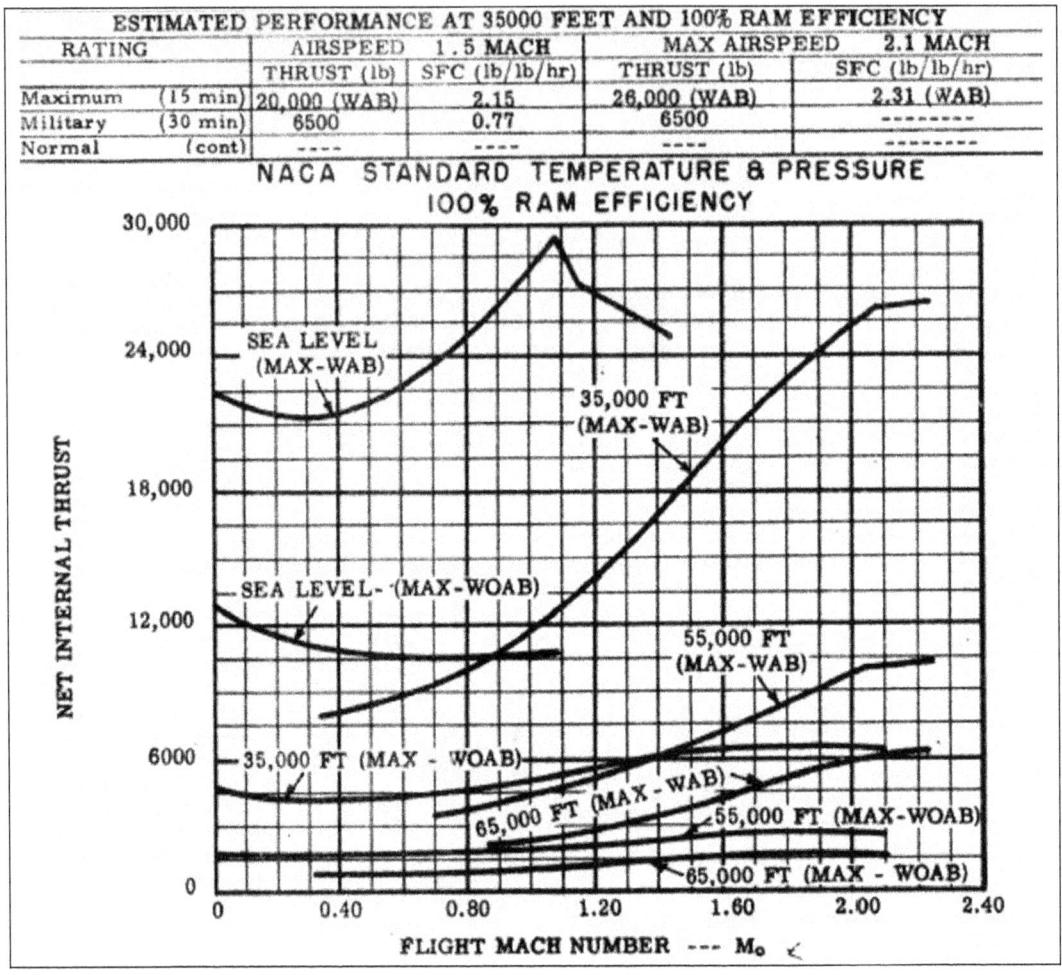

Figure 3.12. Diagram showing multiple data sets in tabular – Estimated Performance at 35,000 ft. and 100% Ram (Ramjet) Efficiency – and graph – NACA Standard Temperature & Pressure 100% Ram (ramjet) Efficiency – formats. AECS YJ67-W-3, 1953

Armament capacity remained the same as for the 1951 AP-57 iteration – 36 x 2.75 in. (~6.985 cm) unguided FFAR (Folding Fin Aircraft Rocket) and 6 x XGAR-1A (formerly XAAM-2) guided air to air missiles. The FFAR, like the missile armament, were now carried on retractable launchers in a weapon bay. As with the 1951 AP-57 design iteration, the missiles would be carried on racks within the internal weapon bays, accessed through the aircraft central-forward fuselage underside, aft of the cockpit area. (CS XF-103, 1954).

The Hughes GAR-1 Falcon was specified as the primary armament. In its earliest guise the GAR-1 program was initiated in March 1947. As a guided air to air missile the program took on heightened importance in March 1948. The first successful test against an airborne target was conducted in 1952 – from 1956 the GAR-1 would go on to constitute the missile armament of the Convair F-102, the winner of the MX-1554 competition (CS GAR-1, 1954).

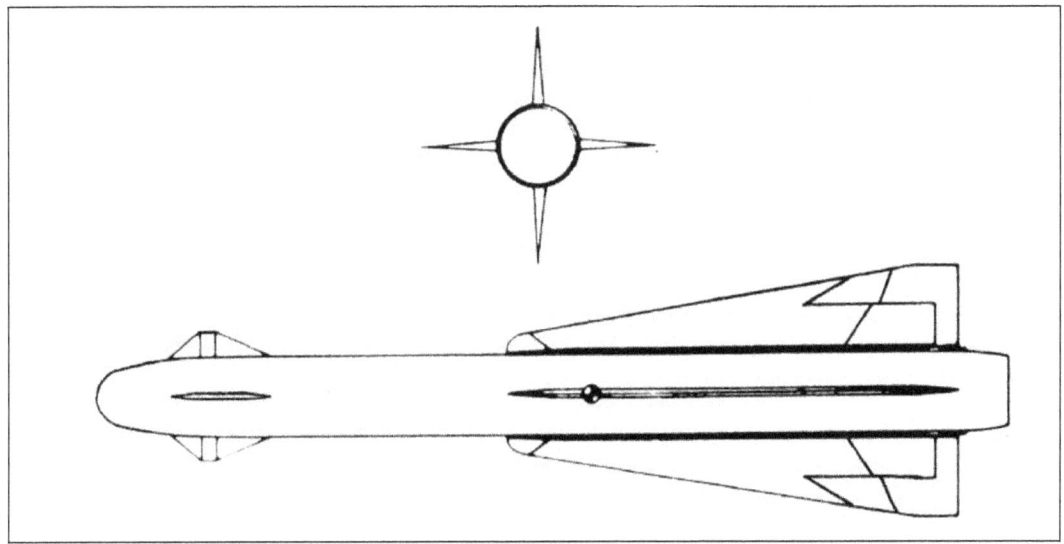

Figure 3.13. Port side-on and frontal aspect views general arrangement drawing of the Hughes GAR-1. CS GAR-1, 1954

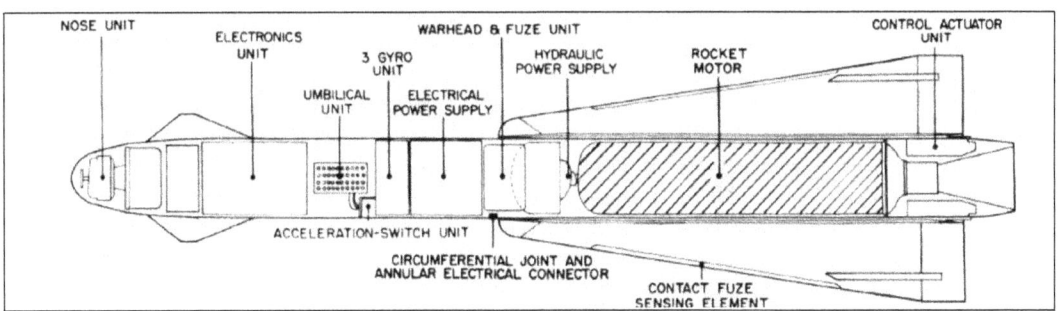

Figure 3.14. Cutaway drawing of the GAR-1 air to air missile, detailing the major sections. SMC GAR-1, 1959

GAR-1 length was 77.8 in (~197.612 cm); span, 20.0 in (~50.8 cm); height, 20.0 in (~50.8 cm) with hydraulic control of surfaces implemented on signals from the seeker head. Although later variants of the GAR-1 would employ the T56 or M9 solid rocket motors the variant associated with the XF-103 was specified to employ the T47 solid rocket motor with a thrust rating of 4.600 lb. (~2086.5 kg) over a 1.3 second duration, consuming the 31 lb. (~14.061 kg) of Thiokol Chemical Corporation Base fuel. The missile had a specified launch weight of 127 lb. (~57.6 kg), this reducing to 96 lb. (~43.4 kg) at rocket motor burnout once the 31 lb. of fuel had been consumed. The missile was not guided during the boost phase, but employed mid-course and terminal phase guidance through the onboard semi-active X-Band Pulse Radar and 'Proportional Navigation' (CS GAR-1, 1954). The GAR-1 was designed to be employed against large airborne targets such as strategic bombers, the target to be destroyed or damaged by an 8 lb. (~3.62 kg) blast fragmentation warhead (CS GAR-1, 1954).

The GAR-1 was launched from wingtip launch rails on the Northrop F-89 subsonic interceptor and launched from internal missile bays on the F-102, this latter method, as noted above, being specified for the XF-103. On the F-102 a time of ~20 seconds from target detection to missile launch was considered the norm (CS GAR-1, 1954), a similar time period being expected for the XF-103.

The GAR-1 had an effective range of 5,000-25,000 ft. (~1524-7620 m) at altitudes up to 60,000 ft. (~18288 m), velocity being ~2,000 ft. (~609.6 m)/second above the velocity of the launch platform. Expected missile accuracy was rather poor, as was the case for all radar guided missiles of the period – 'P_K – .50 to .95' for a full six missile salvo against subsonic and low supersonic bomber aircraft (CS GAR-1, 1954). Salvo launch of six missiles, necessitated through the poor hit expectancy, would consume the entire load of guided missiles against a single target. Secondary targets, or the primary target, if not destroyed by the GAR-1 missile salvo, would have been engaged with the battery of 2.75 in FFAR.

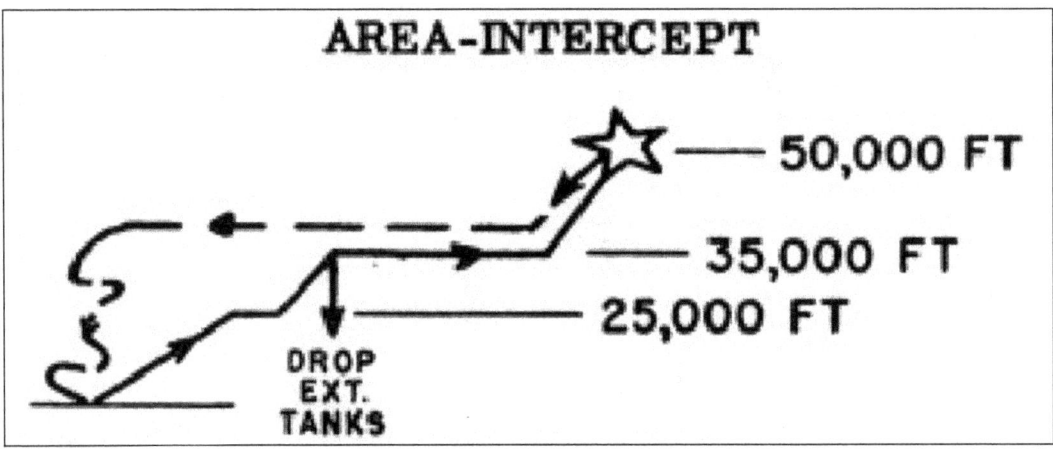

Figure 3.15. Basics parameters of the area intercept mission as defined for the MX-1554(A) Republic XF-103 (AP-57) design iteration of 1954. CS XF-103, 1954

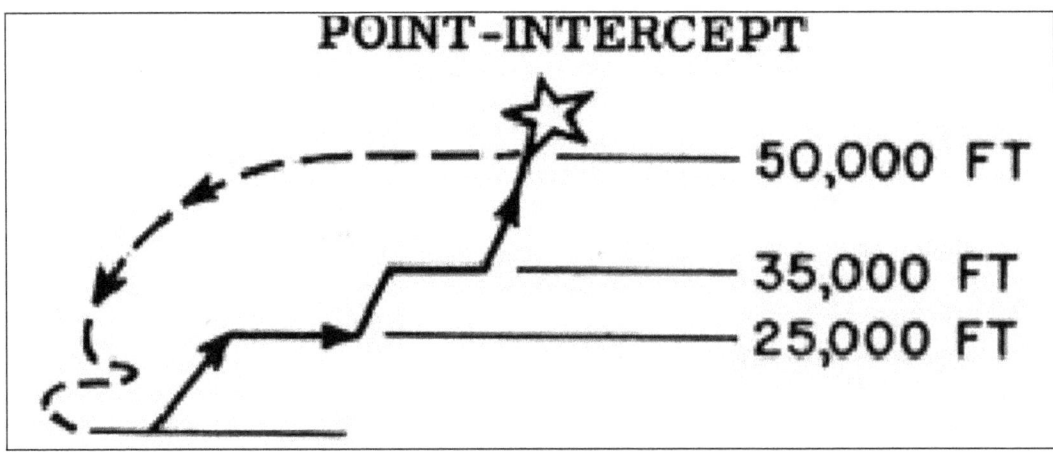

Figure 3.16. XF-103 1954 point-interception basic parameters. CS XF-103, 1954

Figure 3.17. Mock-up of the XF-103, close in detail to the MX-1554(A) Republic Model AP-57 design iteration of 1954. NMUSAF

Figure 3.18. Model of the MX-1554(A) Republic XF-103 (Model AP-57) design iteration of 1954. Republic Archives

For an area interception mission the XF-103 design iteration of 1954 would have required a non-assisted ground run of 3,680 ft. (~1121.66 m) – an increase of 670 ft. (~204 m) over that required for the 1951 AP-57 – and 5,070 ft. (~1545 m) to reach an altitude of 50 ft. (~15.24 m) – an increase of 470 ft. (~143.26 m) over that required by the 1951 AP-57. Combat speed on a point interception was put at 1724 knots (~3193 km/h) at an altitude of 50,000 ft. (~15240 m) and maximum ramjet power. This was the projected maximum speed at altitudes between 45,000 ft. (~13411 m) and 70,000 ft. (~21336 m) under ramjet power (CS XF-103, 1954).

At point interception take-off weight the aircraft was to be capable of take-off, a 25,100 fpm (~7650.4 m/pm (metres per minute)) climb rate at sea level at maximum turbojet power increasing to 41,000 fpm (~12527.2 m/pm) on maximum ramjet power (equivalent sea level conditions). Time to climb from sea level to 50,000 ft. (~15240 m) altitude was put at 7.1 minutes at point interception take-off weight (the climb would have employed the turbojet to an altitude of 35,000 ft. (~10668 m) before switching to ramjet power for the remainder of the climb). Ceiling on a point interception was put at 69,600 ft. (~21214 m) at 100 fpm (~30.48 m/pm) and 69,200 ft. (~21092 m) at maximum ramjet power (CS XF-103, 1954).

Ferry range was put at 1,343 nm (~2487 km) at an average speed of 545 knots (~1009 km/h) in a flight time of 2.52 hours (take-off weight value provided was 41,791 lb. (~18956 kg). Mission time for a point interception at 59,000 ft. (~17938.2 m) altitude = 12.1 minutes. Mission time for an area interception at a distance of 213 nm (~394 km) and average speed of 589 knots (~1091 km/h) was 0.83 hours. Stalling speed on an area intercept mission, in power-off landing configuration, was 156 knots (289 km/h) (CS XF-103, 1954).

Mission scenario I – The XF-103 design iteration of 1954 was to be capable of taking off and, under maximum power, climbing to an altitude of 25,000 ft. (~7620 m) and accelerate to a speed of 1130 knots (~2093 km/h). Under maximum power, accelerate to a speed of 1200 knots (~2224 km/h) and climb to an altitude of 35,000 ft. (~10668 m). The aircraft would then accelerate, under maximum power, to a speed of 1285 knots (~2380 km/h) at 35,000 ft. – a further maximum power acceleration brought speed to 1438 knots (~2663 km/h) at 35,000 ft. followed by acceleration to 1724 knots (~3193 km/h) and climb to 45,000 ft. (~13716 m) under ramjet power. A further step climb was conducted, under ramjet power, to 50,000 ft. (~15240 m) altitude to conduct a 5 minute combat phase under partial ramjet power (the term partial refers to the fact that at altitudes above 14,000 ft. (~4267 m) the maximum attainable speed of the XF-103 would have been determined by the strength limitations imposed by the airframe and engine, excess thrust being retained for combat maneuvering and additional climb). Additional mission time allowances included 2 minutes at normal power, 1 minute at maximum power for engine run-up and ground taxiing and a 20 minutes loiter at sea level (SAC XF-103, 1954).

Radius Mission Scenario II – The XF-103 design iteration of 1954 was to be capable of taking off and, under maximum power, climbing to an altitude of 25,000 ft. (~7620 m) for cruise at military power at that altitude. It would then climb, at long-range speeds, to an altitude of 35,000 ft. (~10668 m) before accelerating at maximum ramjet power to a speed of 1438 knots (~2663 km/h). A further step climb/acceleration, fist to 45,000 ft. (~15716 m)/1724 knots (~3193 km/h) under maximum ramjet power then to 50,000 ft. (~15240 m), for the 5 minute combat phase at that altitude under partial ramjet power. Following the combat phase the aircraft would descend to an altitude of 35,000 ft. (~10668 m) for the return cruise flight back to base. A 20 minute loiter phase would be conducted at sea level before the final return to base. Additional mission time allowances included a 2 minute period at normal power, a 1 minute period at maximum power for engine run-up and ground taxiing and a 20 minute period for loiter at sea level. The mission range/time values included the 5 minutes allocated for the combat phase and the 20 minute sea level loiter allowance (SAC XF-103, 1954).

Mission scenario III (Design mission to meet the requirement set out for the MX-1554 interceptor performance, issued to all participating design houses) – Would be as for mission scenario I with the exception that fuel allowances did not take into consideration a 5% consumption calculated for the take-off and acceleration phases and that the combat phase would be conducted at an altitude of 60,000 ft. (~18288 m) rather than the 50,000 ft. (~15240 m) altitude of mission scenario I. Mission scenario III also made allowance for a 15 minute loiter period at an altitude of 35,000 ft. (~10668 m) and acceleration from landing speed to a speed twice as high, and a further allowance for a 10 minute loiter at sea level (SAC XF-103, 1954).

Range Mission IV (Design mission to meet the requirement set out for the MX-1554 interceptor, issued to all participating design houses) – The XF-103 design iteration of 1954 was to be capable of taking off and, under military power, climb to an altitude of 25,000 ft. (~7620 m) for cruise at military power at that altitude before climbing, under military power, to an altitude of 30,000 ft. (~9144 m) where external fuel tanks would be jettisoned. The aircraft would then cruise at an altitude of 30,000 ft. at optimum extended range speed until an altitude of 35,000 ft. (~10668 m) was exceeded. Additional mission range allowances included a 2 minute period at normal power and a 1 minute period at maximum power for engine run-up and ground taxiing, a 20 minute period for loiter at sea level and a 5% fuel reserve (SAC XF-103, 1954). The above mission scenarios were finalised in July 1953.

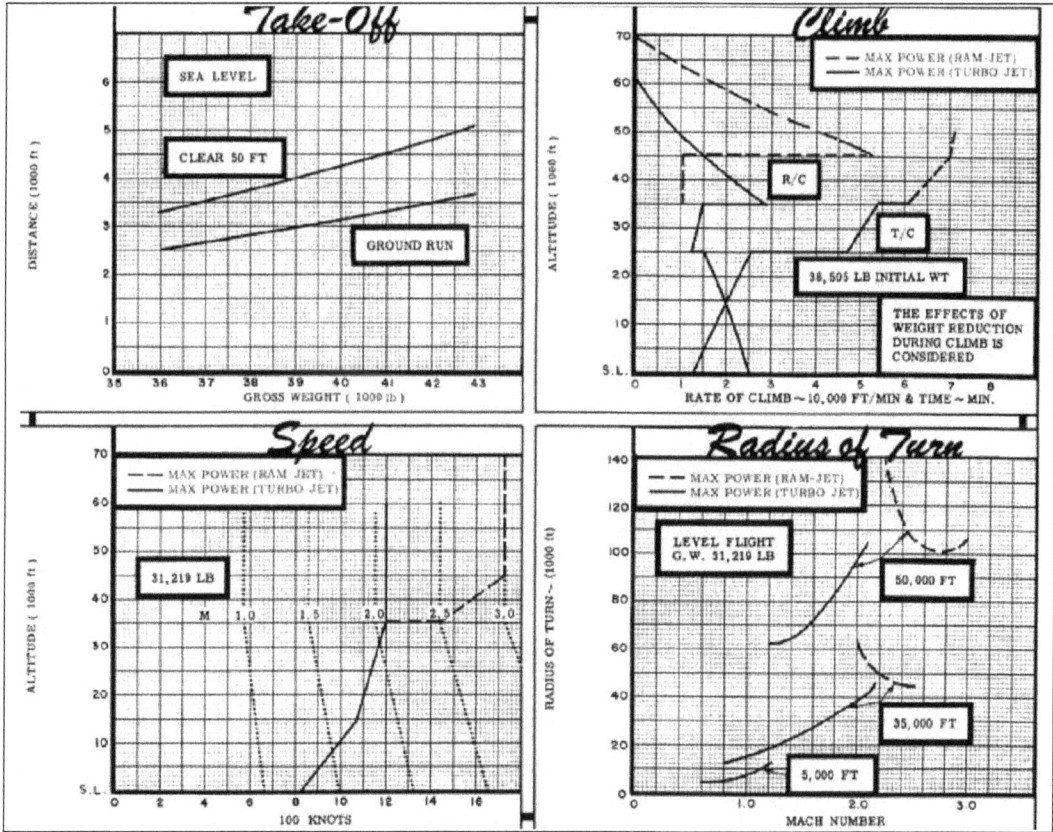

Figure 3.19. Quartet of graphs showing the various performance characteristics of the MX-1554(A) Republic XF-103 (AP-57) design iteration of 1954, based on contractor data for take-off, climb, speed and radius performance. SAC XF-103, 1954

Table 3.5. XF-103 design iteration of 1954 Loading and performance – typical mission

Conditions	Point	Area	local AD	General AD	Ferry
Take-Off Weight .	38,505 lb.	43.864 lb.	37,980 lb.	42,245 lb.	
Fuel at 6.5 lb./gal)	11,700 lb.	15,429 lb.[1]	11,175 lb.	14,810 lb.	
Payload (rockets)[2]	1,504 lb.	1,504 lb.	1,504 lb.	1,504 lb.	1,504 lb.
Wing loading	96 lb./ft^2	106.9 lb./ft^2	94.7 lb./ft^2.	105.3lb./ft^2	104.2 lb./ft^2
Take-off run, sea level[3]	2,900 ft.	3,680 ft.	3,810 ft.	3,550 ft.	3,450 ft.
Take-off to clear 50 ft.[4]	3,880 ft.	5,070 ft.	3,750 ft.	4,880 ft.	4,750 ft.
Rate of climb at SL[5]	25,100 fpm	18,800 fpm	25,800 fpm	19,100 fpm	4,710 fpm[6]
Climb, SL-40,000 ft.[7]	3.9 minutes[8]	4.0 minutes	3.8 minutes[9]	3.5 minutes	6.9 minutes[10]
Climb, SL-50,000 ft.[11]	6.3 minutes[12]		6.1 minutes[12A]		10.5 minutes[13]
Climb, SL-40,000 ft.[14]	6.5 minutes		6.3 minutes		
Climb, SL-50,000 ft.[15]	7.1 minutes		6.9 minutes		
Ceiling (100 fpm)	69,000 ft.[16]	44,500 ft.	70,000 ft.	45,000 ft.	33,000 ft.
Combat range					1,343 nm
Combat radius		213 nm		375 nm	
Average cruise speed		589 nm		544 nm	545 nm
Initial cruise altitude		25,000 ft.		25,000 ft.	25,000 ft.
Final cruise altitude		35,000 ft.		35,000 ft.	35,000 ft.
Total mission time[17]		0.20 hours		0.21 hours	
Interception altitude		50,000 ft.		60,000 ft.	
Combat weight	31,219 lb.	33,764 lb.	30.455 lb.	32,245 lb.	27,512 lb.
Combat altitude	50,000 ft.	60,000 ft.	60,000 ft.	60,000 ft.	35,000 ft.
Combat speed[18]	1724 knots	1724 knots	1724 knots	1724 knots	1438 knots
Combat climb[19]	41,000 fpm	37,500 fpm	42,000 fpm	49,000 fpm	49,000 fpm
Com ceiling (500 fpm)[20]	69,200 ft.	67,600 ft.	69,600 ft.	68,500 ft.	71,600 ft.
Com ceiling (100 fpm)[21]	69,400 ft.	67,800 ft.	69,800 ft.	68,700 ft.	71,800 ft.
Max climb rate at SL	30,000 fpm	27,900 fpm	30,700 fpm	29,200 fpm	34,100 fpm
Max speed, 45-70,000 ft.	1724 knots	1724 knots	1724 knots	1724 knots	1724 knots
Landing weight	26,687 lb.	27,490 lb.	26,876 lb.	26,876 lb.	27,512 lb.
Ground roll at SL[22]	2,720 ft.	2,900 ft.	2,760 lb.	2,760 lb.	2.910 ft.
Land distance, 50 ft.[23]	4,080 ft.	4,310 ft.	4,120 ft.	4,120 ft.	4.320 ft.

[1] With 287 gal external fuel tanks
[2] 6 x XGAR-1A guided missile and 36 x 2.75 inch unguided air to air rockets
[3] Maximum turbojet power
[4] Maximum turbojet power
[5] SL (Sea Level). Maximum turbojet power. Includes allowance for reducing weight through ground operations and the ascent
[6] Military power
[7] Maximum turbojet power. Includes allowance for reducing weight through ground operations and the ascent
[8] Includes take-off and acceleration to optimum climb speed
[9] Includes take-off and acceleration to optimum climb speed
[10] Military power. Time to 20,000 ft.
[11] Maximum turbojet power. Includes allowance for reducing weight through ground operations and the ascent
[12] And 12A. Includes take-off and acceleration to optimum climb speed – acceleration to 1200 knots
[13] Military power. Time to 25,000 ft.
[14] Includes allowance for reducing weight through ground operations and the ascent from standing start to max speed at altitude
[15] Includes allowance for reducing weight through ground operations and the ascent from standing start to max speed at altitude
[16] Maximum ramjet power – Maximum turbojet power – military power
[17] These values include the time required for take-off and acceleration to the optimum climb speed
[18] Maximum ramjet power
[19] Maximum ramjet power
[20] Com = combat. Maximum ramjet power
[21] Com = combat. Maximum ramjet power
[22] Employing 16 ft. ring-slot landing drag parachute
[23] From altitude of 50 ft. Employing 16 ft. ring-slot landing drag parachute

4

XF-103 RESEARCH INTERCEPTOR DESIGN ITERATION OF JULY 1957

By the time details of the next design iteration of the XF-103 were released in July 1957, the MX-1554 had become the domain of the F-102, which was firmly established in USAF (United States Air Force) service. No longer feeding the MX-1554 program, the XF-103 program transformed from that of proving a design for operational service to that of an experimental program intended to prove technologies that could be applicable to future generation interceptors. Two development aircraft were ordered to be built – a reduction from the three planned, but not realised, for the 1954 design iteration. The first XF-103 was now scheduled to conduct its maiden flight around March 1959 and the second was scheduled to follow the first into the air around November that year (CS XF-103, 1957).

No longer intended to form the basis of an operational interceptor platform, the major research areas for the XF-103 were: 1. Prove the practicability of the double (dual)-cycle YJ67-W-3/XRJ55-W-1 power plant in flight. 2. Provide data on reliability of aircraft systems at high supersonic flight (up to Mach 3) and high altitudes (in excess of 50,000 ft. (~15240 m). 3. Investigate the practicability of the pilot escape capsule (this ejected downward through the underside of the aircraft) when flying at high supersonic speed. 4. Determine whether or not titanium was an effective material for use in aircraft and missile construction. 5. Provide a high speed platform to conduct flight research into interceptor aircraft tactics at high supersonic speeds (up to Mach 3) (CS XF-103, 1957).

Among the main design features for the titanium structure XF-103 design iteration of 1957 was the retention of the NACA 65A-003 delta wing section of the 1951 & 1954 design iterations, incorporating double slotted flaps. Wing area, like that of its paper forebears, was 401 sq. ft. (~122.22 m^2) and aspect ratio was 3.2. A large stabilising empennage was added to the rear underside. The aircraft remained a single crew design with a pilot escape capsule housed within a submerged section with a periscope to provide a forward view; manoeuvring stabiliser; a liquid oxygen system and a hydraulic/electric system powered by an air turbine (CS XF-103, 1957). The

Wright YJ67-W-3 axial flow turbojet, with independent afterburner section functioning as a ramjet, fed air through a variable area ram air intake. Turbojet power would be employed at speeds up to Mach 2.1 when the transition to ramjet power would take place (CS XF-103, 1957). Engine weights, dimensions and ratings changed, at times significantly, as the design iterations evolved. See Table 4.3 & 4.4.

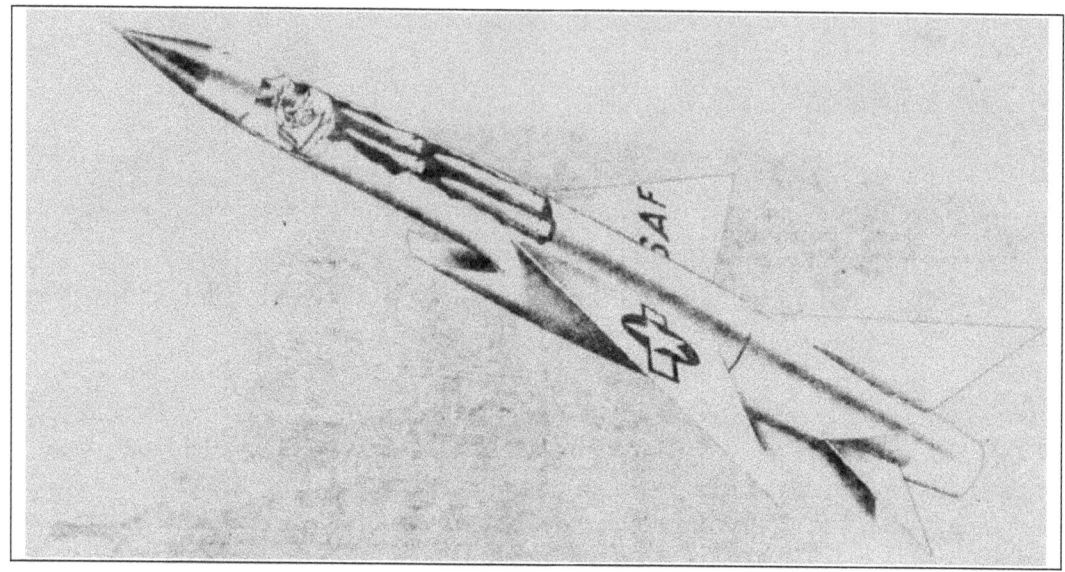

Figure 4.1. Artist rendering of the Republic XF-103 design iteration of 1957. The ghosted forward section shows, from fore to aft, the electronics bay, pressurised pilots compartment and what appears to be weapons bays. Note: The 1957 XF-103 design iteration was intended purely as a research design with no provision for missiles/rockets, the weapon bays were allocated for fuel storage. SAC XF-103, 1957

The 1957 XF-103 design followed the convention that the electronics were located in the aircraft nose section with the pilot (housed in an escape capsule) aft of the electronics bay with the forward undercarriage bay and forward fuel tanks located aft of the pilot compartment. The air inlet and transition section was located more or less at the central fuselage section with the power plant compartment behind and the afterburner/ramjet exit nozzle at the extreme rear below the vertical tail section. Further fuel tankage was located in the upper central and aft fuselage sections with the rear undercarriage unit located below the power plant compartment in the rear fuselage section (CS XF-103, 1957).

Documentation dated 1 July 1957 showed a design 81.9 ft. (~24.96 m) in length (an increase of 5.1 ft. (~15.54 m) over the 1954 XF-103 and 8.3 ft. (~2.52 m) over the 1951 AP-57); wingspan 35.8 ft. (~10.9 m) (an increase of 1.4 ft. (0.42 m) over the 1954 XF-103 design and 0.1 ft. more than the 1951 AP-57); height 16.5 ft. (~5 m) (a 1.8 ft. (0.54 m) increase over that of the 1954 XF-103 design iteration, but still 1.2 ft. (~0.36 m) less than that of the 1951 AP-57 design iteration; tread 12.3 ft. (~3.7 m) (an increase of 1 ft. over that of the 1954 XF-103 design iteration and 1.1 ft. (~0.33 m) more than that of the 1951 AP-57 design iteration (CS XF-103, 1957).

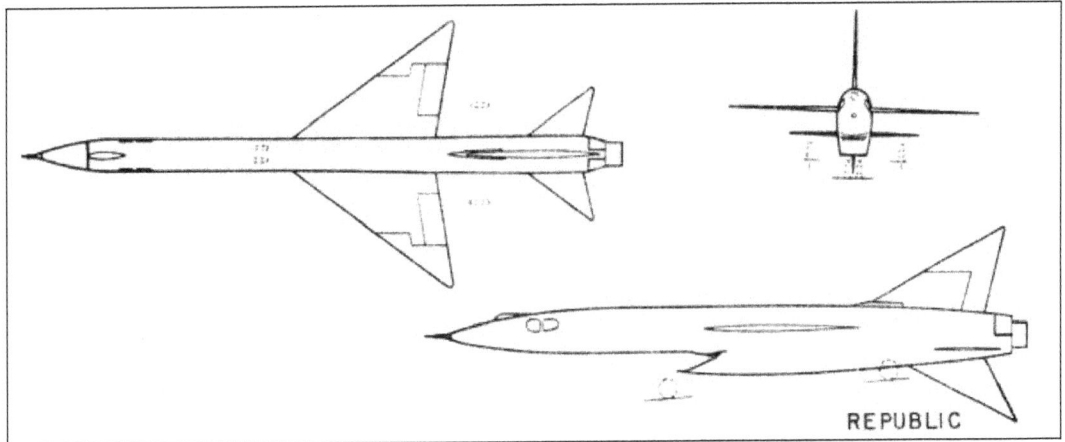

Figure 4.2. Three view general arrangement drawing of the Republic XF-103 design iteration of 1957. SAC XF-103, 1957/Republic Archives

DIMENSIONS
Wing
Span: 35.8 ft. (~10.91 m)
Incidence: 0° (root); 0° (tip)
Dihedral: 0°
Sweepback (leading edge): 55°
Length: 81.9 ft. (~24.96 m)
Height: 18.3 ft. (~5.6 m)
Tread: 12.3 ft. (~3.74 m)

Table 4.1. Basic dimensions of the XF-103 design iteration of 1957. SAC XF-103, 1957

Projected weights for the 1957 XF-103 design were 32,575 lb. (~14776 kg) empty (an increase of 7,626 lb. (~3459 kg) over that of the 1954 XF-103 design iteration and 13,206 lb. (~5990 kg) over that of the 1951 AP-57); 32,970 lb. (~14955 kg) basic; 35,260 lb. (~15993.6 kg) design; 38,200 lb. (~17327 kg) combat; 55,780 lb. (~25301 kg) maximum take-off (limited by undercarriage design) and 36,399 lb. (~16510 kg) maximum landing (limited by undercarriage design) (SAC XF-103, 1957).

WEIGHTS
Empty: 32,575 lb. (~14776 kg) – calculated
Basic: 32,970 lb. (~14955 kg) – calculated
Design: 35,260 lb. (~15993.6 kg)
Combat: 38,200 lb. (~17327 kg) – for research flight
Maximum take-off weight: 55,780 lb. (~25301 kg) – limited by undercarriage design
Maximum landing: 36,399 lb. (~16510 kg) – limited by undercarriage design

Table 4.2. Projected weights of the XF-103 design iteration of 1957. SAC XF-103, 1957

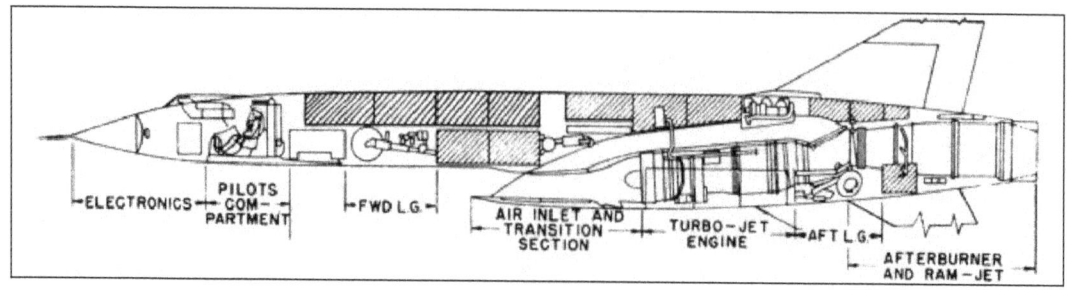

Figure 4.3. Port side-view ghosted graphic showing sections of the Republic XF-103 design iteration of 1957 – fore to aft: Electronic equipment; pilot compartment; forward undercarriage unit; air inlet and transition section; YJ67-W-3 axial flow turbojet engine; aft undercarriage unit and afterburner/ramjet. SAC XF-103, 1957

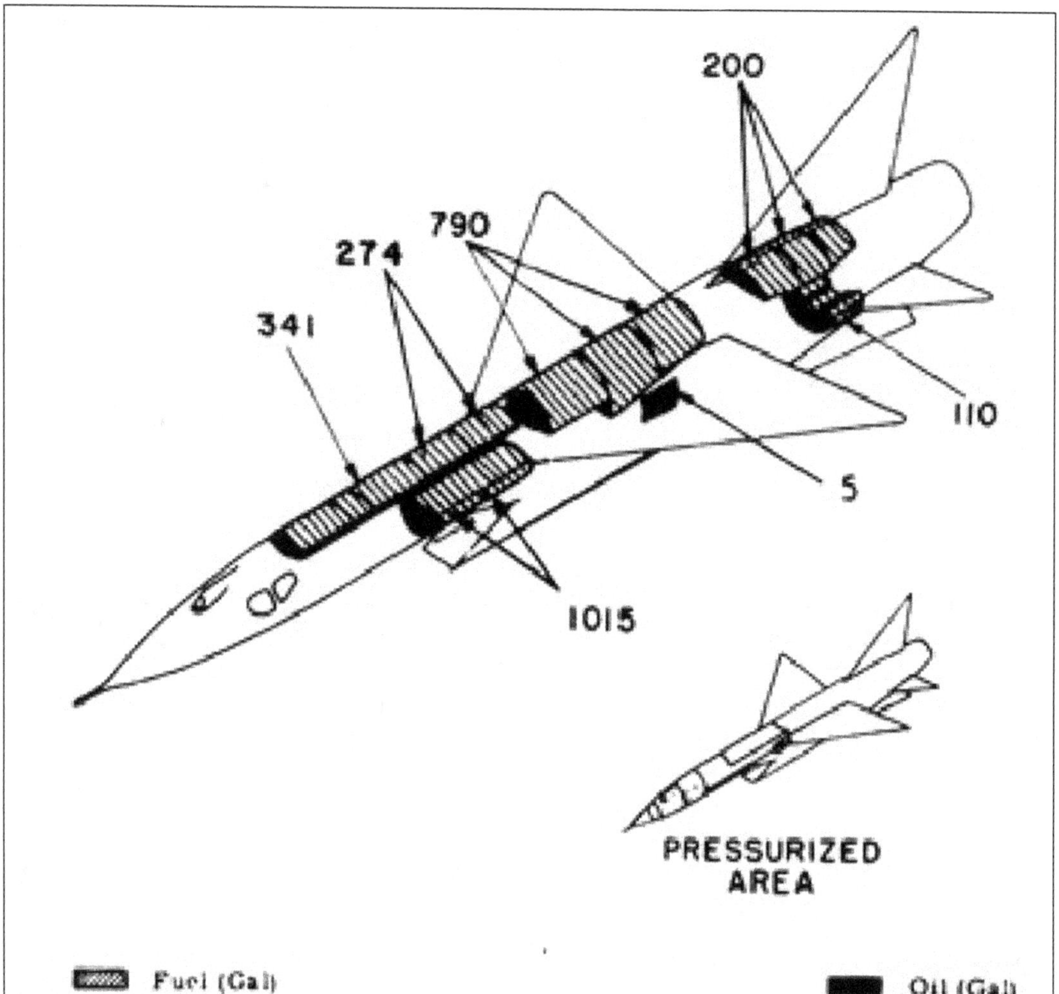

Figure 4.4. Graphic depicting the XF-103 design iteration of 1957 forward section pressurised compartment and the JP-4 Grade fuel and 1015 Grade oil tankage, amounting to 2630 gal and 5 gal respectively. SAC XF-103, 1957

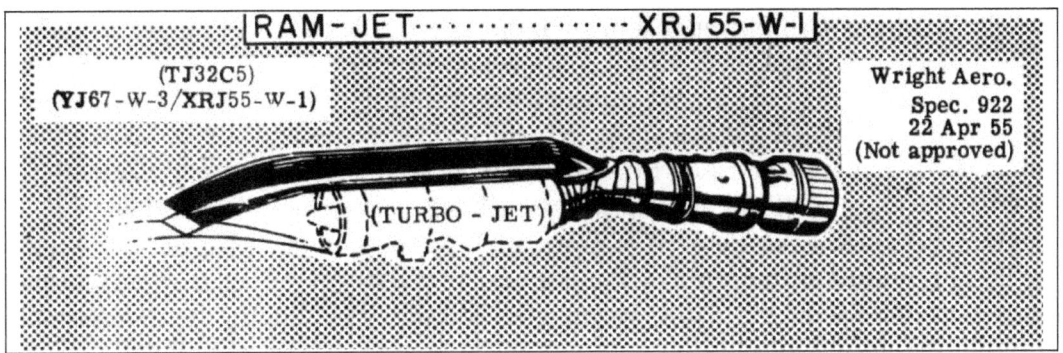

Figure 4.5. Basic layout diagram of the YJ67-W-3/XRJ55-W-1 double (dual)-cycle engine and the air inlet and transition section intended for the XF-103. AECS XRJ55-W-1, 1956

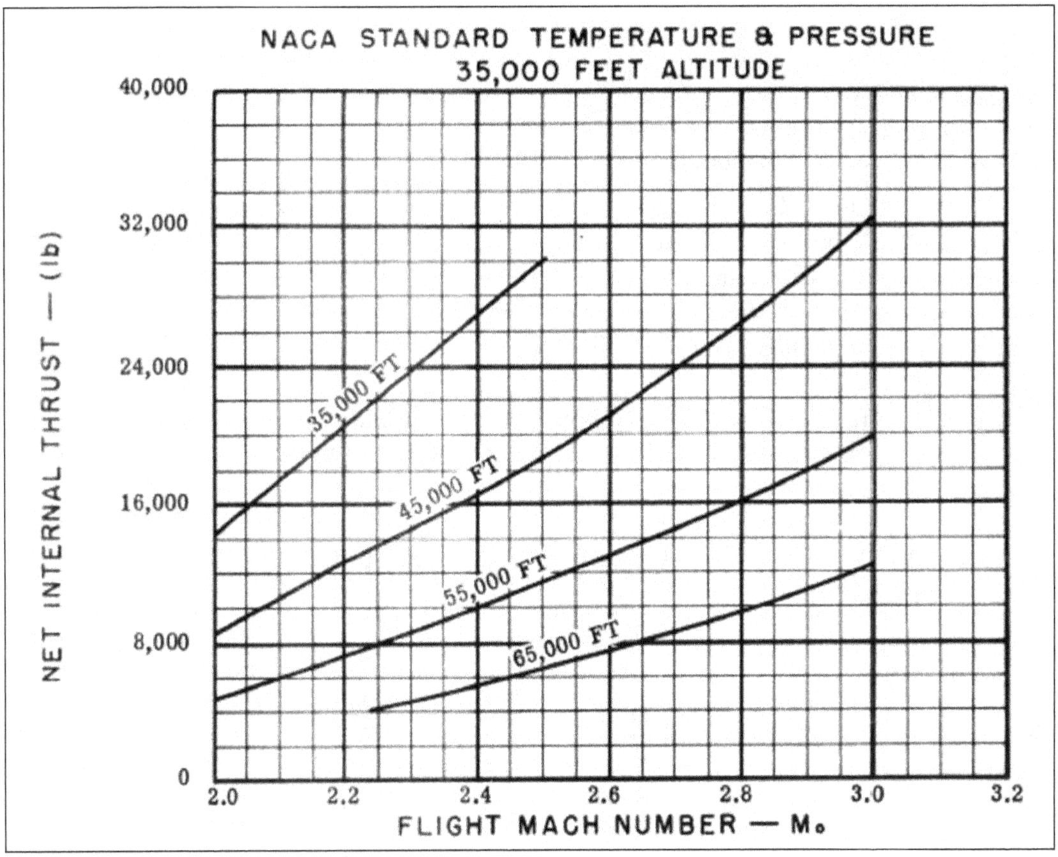

Figure 4.6. Graph showing NACA Standard Temperature & Pressure 100% Ram (ramjet) Efficiency. AECS XRJ55-W-1, 1956

Intended as a research aircraft, the 1957 design lacked any provision for the carriage of armament – this was six GAR-1A guided missiles and 36 x 2.76 in unguided rockets in the previous design iterations of 1951 & 1954 (SAC XF-103,

1957). The lack of an operational mission dictated the deletion of the Hughes MX-1179 Electronic Control System. The major electronics suit consisted of an AN/ARC-34 UHF (Ultra High Frequency) command system, AN/AIC-10 intercom and an AN/URC-4 rescue radio (SAC XF-103, 1957).

Fuel capacity was increased from the 2240 gal of the XF-103 design iteration of 1954 to 2630 gal of JP-4-Grade fuel. The fuel tank arrangement was also altered to utilise space freed up by deletion of the missile and rocket armament. Now, 1530 gal would be housed in three forward fuselage tanks; 790 gal would be housed in a central fuselage tank and 310 gal would be housed in two aft fuselage tanks. Oil capacity was increased to 5 gal of 1015 Grade housed in a single tank in the fuselage (SAC XF-103, 1957).

Wright YJ67-W-3/XRJ55-W-1 double (dual)-cycle power plant – afterburner operates as a ramjet

No: 1
Engine Spec No: 922D
Type: Double (Dual)-Cycle, Axial
Length: 534.0 in. (~1356.36 cm)
Diameter: 56.0 in. (~142.24 cm)
Weight (dry): 7,886 lb. (~3577 kg)
Tail pipe/Nozzle type: Variable Area
Augmentation: Afterburner. Afterburner was to be used independently as a ramjet when air was by-passed around the turbojet

---

Table 4.3. Wright YJ67-W-3/XRJ55-W-1 double (dual)-cycle power plant basic specification for the XF-103 design iteration of 1957. AECS XRJ55-W-1, 1956 & SAC XF-103, 1957

Wright YJ67-W-3/XRJ55-W-1 double (dual)-cycle power plant – afterburner operates as a ramjet

Turbojet ratings

S.L. Static	Thrust, lb.	RPM	Minutes
Maximum	22,100 (afterburner)	6350/8170	5
Military	13,950	6350/8170	30
Normal	12,150	6350/7925	Cont.

Ramjet design Mach range: 2.24-3.0
Ramjet altitude range: 35,000 ft. (~10668 m)-76,000 ft. (~23165 m)
Thrust 37,400 lb. (~16964 kg)

Table 4.4. Wright YJ67-W-3/XRJ55-W-1 double (dual)-cycle power plant ratings for the XF-103 design iteration of 1957. SAC XF-103, 1957

Loading and Performance – Typical Mission

CONDITIONS	RESEARCH MISSION
Take-off weight	51,267 lb.
Fuel at 6.5 lb./gal (JP-4)	17,745 lb.
Payload	None
Wing loading	127.8 lb./sq. ft.
Stall speed (power off)	175.1 knots
Take-off run, sea level[2-8]	7,140 ft.
Take-off run with assisted take-off	N/A. Then under development
Take-off to clear 50 ft.[2-8]	14,200 ft.
Rate of climb at sea level[2-6]	19,150 fpm
Climb from sea level-35,000 ft.[2-4-6]	10.84 minutes
Climb from sea level-60,000 ft.[2-4-5-6]	21.40 minutes
Ceiling (100 fpm)[2-7]	50,000 ft.
Average cruise speed	531 knots
Return cruise altitude	30,000 ft.
Total mission time	0.76 hours
Total test time[4]	2.5 minutes[10]
Test altitude	60,000 ft.
Combat Weight	38,200 lb.
Combat altitude	60,000 ft.
Combat speed[1]	1720 knots (Mach 3)
Combat climb[1]	16,200 fpm
Combat ceiling (500 fpm)[1]	69,570 ft.
Combat ceiling (100 fpm)[1]	68,830 ft.
Maximum climb rate at sea level[2]	23,900 fpm
Maximum speed at 47,500-70,000 ft.[1]	1720 knots (Mach 3)
Basic speed at 50,000 ft.[1]	1720 knots (Mach 3)
Landing weight	35,035 lb.
Ground roll at sea level	4,130 ft.
Total landing distance from 50 ft.	5,410 ft.

2-8 Turbojet power. Take-off for an altitude of 2,300 ft. at a day temperature of 59° Fahrenheit
2-6 Turbojet power
2-4-6 Turbojet power. Includes time for take-off and acceleration to climb speed. Includes allowance for ground operation weight reduction through fuel consumption
2-4-5-6 Turbojet power. Includes time for take-off and acceleration to climb speed and acceleration to transition speed. Includes allowance for ground operation weight reduction through fuel consumption
2-7 Turbojet power. At take-off weight
4 Includes time for take-off and acceleration to climb speed
10 Includes 0.5 minutes from 55,000 ft.-60,000 ft. at Mach 3
1 Ramjet power
2 Turbojet power

Table 4.5. Loading and Performance – Typical mission for the XF-103 design iteration of 1957. SAC XF-103, 1957

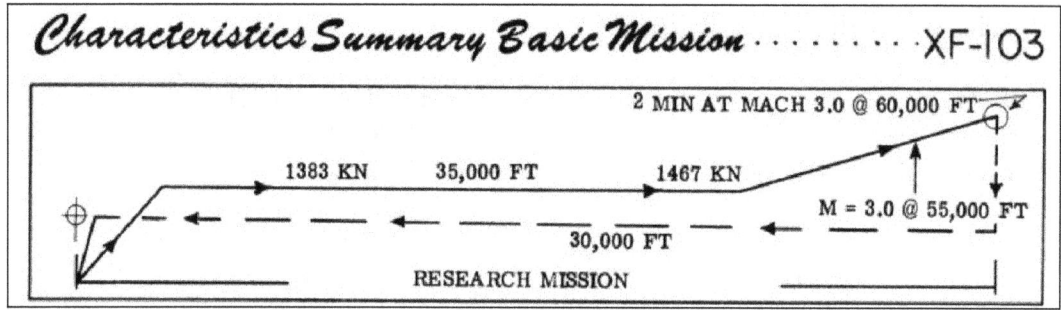

Figure 4.7. Diagram showing the basics parameters of the research mission specified for the XF-103 design iteration of 1957. CS XF-103, 1957

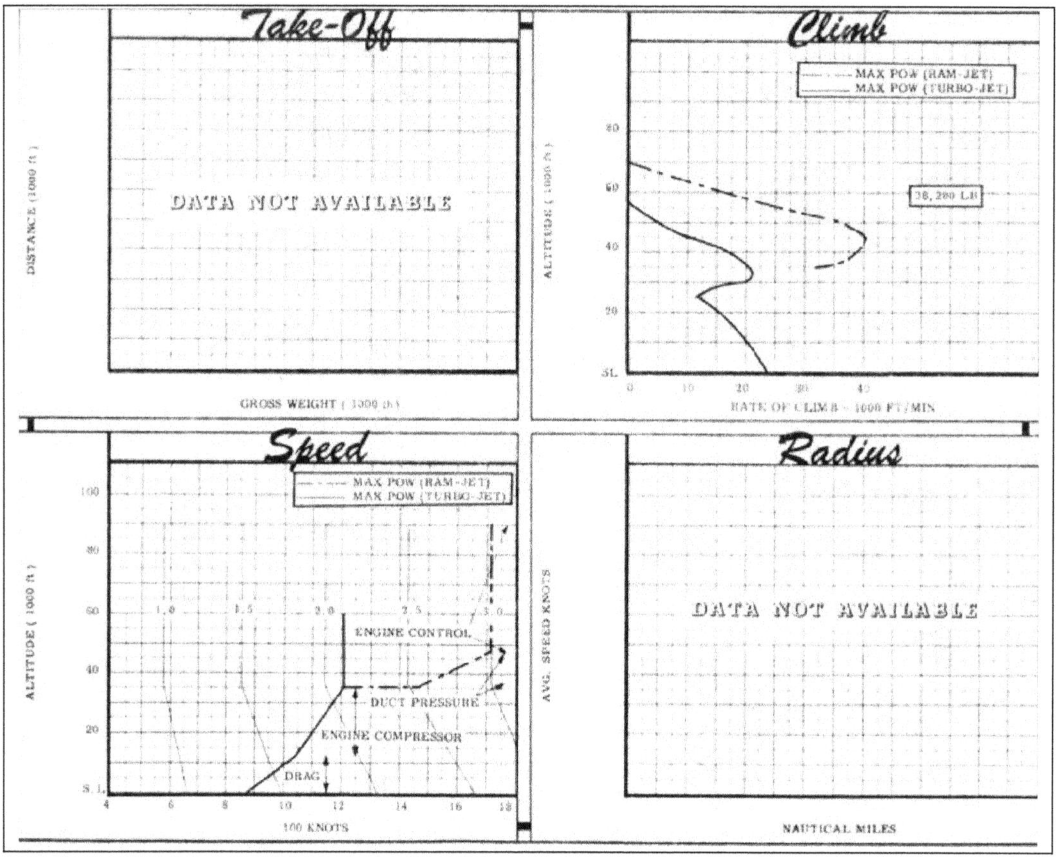

Figure 4.8. Quartet of graphs showing the various performance traits for the XF-103 design iteration of 1957 based on contractor data for take-off, climb, speed and radius (this last category being bereft of data). SAC XF-103, 1957

The basic interception mission specified under MIL-C-5011A was not applicable to the 1957 XF-103 design iteration. The standard mission scenario was referred to as the radius mission in which the aircraft would take-off and climb to an altitude of 35,000 ft. (~10668 m) under maximum turbojet power. At this altitude the aircraft would conduct a step acceleration, first to a speed of 1383 knots (~2561 km/h) under maximum turbojet power, then to 1467 knots (~2717 km/h) under ramjet power. The aircraft would climb to an altitude of 60,000 ft. (~18288 m), accelerate to a speed of 1720 knots (~3195 km/h), at which altitude and speed the aircraft would fly for a period of 2 minutes – the test phase was conducted during this part of the flight – before descending to 30,000 ft. (~9144 m) altitude for the cruise flight back to base. Additional mission time/range allowances included a 5 minute period at normal power and a 1 minute period at maximum power for warm-up and ground taxiing, and fuel for a maximum power take-off, acceleration and maximum power climb to 35,000 ft. (~10668 m). Allowance was made for the 2 minute period on ramjet power at an altitude of 60,000 ft. (~18288 m) at a loading of 1.2 g. A reserve fuel allowance of 1,513 lb. (~686 kg) was included for a loiter at sea level of an unstated duration, but probably no more than 20 minutes (SAC XF-103, 1957).

Figure 4.9. Design iterations of the XF-103 nose and cockpit sections with the downward ejecting escape capsule below. The design on the right of photograph – facing – appears characteristic of the XF-103 design iteration of 1957. NMUSAF

The specification for the 1957 XF-103 design iteration, although detailed in Defense Department documentation dated 1 July 1957, was that determined for the XF-103 prototype Number 1, ES-361, dated 15 April 1957 (SAC XF-103, 1957). While the XF-103 was in development, the AMC (Air Material Command) of the USAF conducted a design performance analysis, which indicated an estimated maximum speed of 1438 knots (~2663 km/h), considerably below the 1720 knots

(~3204 km/h) specification put forward by the contractor. The design would have been limited to Mach 3 due to the estimation of excessive turbine inlet air temperature (SAC XF-103, 1957).

The XF-103 program was cancelled in its entirety on 21 August 1957 (notification) and officially terminated in September that year, before any of the two development aircraft had been built. At the same time, the Wright MX-1797 YJ67-W-3/XRJ55-W-1 double (dual)-cycle engine was cancelled. It is estimated that the program had cost $104 million dollars from its inception to cancellation (Knack, 1978). Even as the MX-1554 generation of interceptor concepts was being developed attention was turning to the projected post-1960 threat that was expected to be faced from advanced Soviet bomber developments. These projected threats led to the LRI-X (Long Range-Interceptor Experimental) program. With attention turning to more advanced solutions in the quest to field a Mach 3 interceptor the XF-103 concept had been abandoned through a combination of development difficulties and the fact that the requirement had effectively been superseded by the USAF AIP (Advanced Interceptor Program), Phase I of which had been concluded in September 1955. The AIP would eventually spawn the North American F-108 Mach 3 interceptor program, which, like the XF-103, was destined never to fly (Harkins, 2014).

Figure 4.10. This photograph appears to show a partially completed mock-up of a design most closely related to the XF-103 design iteration of 1957. Among the areas that are incomplete is the afterburner/ramjet nozzle section, which would be expected to protrude from the extreme rear. NMUSAF/Republic archives

GLOSSARY

AD	Air Defence
ADC	Air Defence Command
ADO	Advanced Development Objective
AECS	Aircraft Engine Characteristic Summary
AGARD	Advisory Group for Aerospace Research & Development
AIP	Advanced Interceptor Program
AMC	Air Material Command
cm	centimetre
CONUS	Continental United States
CS	Characteristic summary
ECS	Electronic Control System
F	Fighter
fpm	Feet per minute
ft.	Feet (unit of measurement)
ft.^{2}	Feet squared (unit of measurement)
g	Gravity (1 g = 1 x Earth gravity)
gal	Gallon
GAR	Guided Aircraft Rocket
I	Roman numeral number 1
lb.	Pound (unit of weight)
lb./lb./hr.	pound per pound per hour
ICBM	Intercontinental Ballistic Missile
II	Roman numeral number 2
III	Roman numeral number 3
in.	Inch
IV	Roman numeral number 4
kg	Kilogram
km	Kilometer
km/h	Kilometers per hour
Knots	Nautical Miles per Hour
LRI-X	Long Range-Interceptor-Experimental
m	Metre
m^2	Metre squared
Mach	1 Mach = the speed of sound (this varies with altitude)
Mesosphere	Atmosphere layer that commences above where the stratosphere ends and extends to an altitude of 85 km where the thermosphere begins
MODRF	Ministry of Defence of the Russian Federation
m/pm	Metres per minute
NACA	National Advisory Committee on Aeronautics
NASA	National Aeronautics and Space Administration
NATO	North Atlantic Treaty Organisation
nm	Nautical Mile

NMUSAF	National Museum of the United States Air Force
RPM	Revolutions Per Minute
SAC	Standard Aircraft Characteristics
Sq. ft.	Square feet (unit of measurement)
SMC	Standard Missile Characteristics
Stratosphere	Atmosphere layer commencing just above where the troposphere ends, ~14.5 km, extending to an altitude of ~50 km
USAF	United States Air Force
WADC	Wright Air Development Centre
XAAM	Experimental Air to Air Missile
XF	Experimental Fighter
XGAR	Experimental Guided Aircraft Rocket
10^6	1,000000 (1 million)
~	Approximately equal to (can also be used to mean asymptotically equal)
°	Degree(s)

BIBLIOGRAPHY

Advisory Group for Aerospace Research & Development (1991) 'Air Intakes for High Speed Vehicles', North Atlantic Treaty Organisation

Aircraft Engine Characteristic Summary (1953), 'Turbojet YJ67-W-3', Authority of Secretary of the Air Force

Aircraft Engine Characteristic Summary (1956), 'Ramjet XRJ55-W-1', Authority of Secretary of the Air Force

Avro A Luoma NACA Research Memorandum for USAF (1953), 'Longitudinal Stability and Control Characteristics at Transonic Speeds of a 1/30-Scale Model of the Republic XF-103 Airplane', Langley Aeronautical Laboratory Langley Field, Va, NACA RM SL54H24

Characteristic Summary (1951), 'Fighter Interceptor, 1954 AWI', Wright Air Development Centre, USAF

Characteristic Summary (1954), 'Fighter Interceptor, XF-103', Authority of Secretary of the Air Force

Characteristic Summary (1957), 'Fighter (Research), XF-103', Authority of Secretary of the Air Force

Characteristic Summary (1954) 'Guided Aircraft Rocket GAR-1', Authority of Secretary of the Air Force

Hall, Charles F. NACA Research Memorandum (1953) 'Lift, Drag and Pitching Moment of Low-Aspect-Ratio Wings at Subsonic and Supersonic Speeds'. NACA RM A53A30

Harkins, H. (2007) *USAF Jet Fighters, 1942-1972*, Centurion Publishing, United Kingdom

Harkins, H. (2014) *North American F-108 Rapier*, Centurion Publishing, United Kingdom

Harkins, H. (2016) *Air War over Syria, Tu-160, Tu-95MS & Tu-22M3*, Centurion Publishing, United Kingdom

Harkins, H. (2018) *Sukhoi T-4 Sotka: The Soviet Mach 3+ Hypersonic Missile Carrier/Airborne Reconnaissance System*, Centurion Publishing, United Kingdom

Harkins, H. (2019) *Russia's Strategic Missile Carrier/Bomber Roadmap, 2018-2040*, Centurion Publishing, United Kingdom

Knack, M.S. *Encyclopedia of USAF Aircraft & Missile System, Post World War II Fighters'*, Washington D.C.: Office of Air Force History, 1978

Lockwood, Vernard E., Luoma, Avor A. & Solomon, Martin (1953) 'Stability and Control Characteristics at High Subsonic Speeds of a 1/30-Scale Model of the MX-1554A Design, NACA RM SL53K12a

Lockwood, Vernard E. & Solomon, Martin, NACA Research Memorandum for USAF (1953) 'Stability and Control Characteristics at Low Speed of a 1/10-Scale Model of MX-1554A Design, NACA RM SL53A05

3M basic characteristic, Monino

3M historical data, Myasishchev

M4 basic characteristic, Myasishchev

M4 basic characteristic, Myasishchev

M4 historical data, Myasishchev

M-50 basic characteristic, Monino

M-50 basic characteristic, Myasishchev

M-50 historical data, Myasishchev

NACA Research Memorandum for USAF (1953), 'Wind-Tunnel Investigation of a 1/60-scale model of the Republic MX-1554 Airplane at a Mach Number of 2.85', Ames Aeronautical Laboratory Moffet Field, California

Smith, Willard G, NACA Research Memorandum (1953) 'Wind-Tunnel Investigation of 1/15-Scale Model of Republic MX-1554 Airplane at Mach numbers of 1.45 and 1.90', NACA RM SA53C17

Standard Aircraft Characteristic (1951), '1954 AW-1 Model AP-57', Wright Air Development Centre, USAF

Standard Aircraft Characteristic (1954), 'XF-103', Authority of Secretary of the Air Force

Standard Aircraft Characteristic (1957), 'XF-103', Authority of Secretary of the Air

Force

Standard Missile Characteristics (1959) 'GAR-1 Falcon', Secretariat of the Air Force

Tu-4 basic characteristic, PJSC Tupolev

Tu-4 basic characteristic, Monino Air Museum

Tu-16 basic characteristic, PJSC Tupolev

Tu-16 basic characteristic, Monino

Tu-22 basic characteristic, PJSC Tupolev

Tu-22 basic characteristic, Monino

Wright, Ray H. & Ward, Vernon G, NACA Research Memorandum (1948) 'NACA Transonic Wind-Tunnel Test Sections', NACA RM L8J06

Untitled historical data relating to Soviet Union's early nuclear bomb tests – 1949 to 1951, Ministry of Defence of the Russian Federation archives

ABOUT THE AUTHOR

Hugh Harkins FRAS is a historian and author with an extensive research background in astro/geophysics and studies/research in the wider scientific, aeronautic, astronautic and nautical technical and historical fields. He is also involved in research in the field of Scottish history, which formed a significant element of an otherwise scientific undergraduate degree. Hugh has published in excess of sixty books; non-fiction and fiction, writing under his given name as well as utilising several pseudonyms. He has also written for several international magazines, whilst his work has been used as reference for many other projects ranging from the aviation industry, international news corporations and film media to encyclopaedias, museum exhibits and the computer gaming industry. Hugh is a member of the Institute of Physics and is an elected Fellow of the Royal Astronomical Society. He currently resides in his native Scotland. Other titles by the author include:

Russia's Coastal Missile Shield - Bal-E & Bastion Mobile Coastal Cruise Missile Complexes
Iskander - Mobile Tactical Aero-Ballistic/Cruise Missile Complex
Orbital/Fractional Orbit Bombardment System - The Soviet Globalnaya Raketa
Counter-Space Defence Co-Orbital Satellite Fighter
Russia's Strategic Missile Carrier/Bomber Roadmap 2018-2040 – PAK DA, Tu-160M2, Tu-95MSM & Tu-22M3M
Sukhoi T-50/PAK FA - Russia's 5th Generation 'Stealth' Fighter
Sukhoi Su-35S 'Flanker' E - Russia's 4++ Generation Super-Manoeuvrability Fighter
Sukhoi Su-34 'Fullback'
Sukhoi Su-30MKK/MK2/M2 - Russo Kitashiy Striker from Amur
Soviet Mixed Power Experimental Fighter Aircraft – Piston-Liquid Propellant Rocket Engine/Piston-Ramjet/Piston-Pulsejet & Piston-Compressor Jet Engine Designs of the 1940's
MiG-35/D 'Fulcrum' F – Towards the Fifth Generation
Air War over Syria, Tu-160, Tu-95MS & Tu-22M3 - Cruise Missile and Bombing Strikes on Syria, November 2015-February 2016
Sukhoi Su-27SM(3)/SKM
Russian/Soviet Aircraft Carrier & Carrier Aviation Design & Evolution Volume 1 - Seaplane Carriers, Project 71/72, Graf Zeppelin, Project 1123 ASW Cruiser & Project 1143-1143.4 Heavy Aircraft Carrying Cruiser
Light Battle Cruisers and the Second Battle of Heligoland Bight
British Battlecruisers of World War 1 - Operational Log, July 1914-June 1915
Eurofighter Typhoon - Storm over Europe
North American F-108 Rapier - Mach 3 Interceptor
Convair YB-60 - Fort Worth Overcast
Boeing X-36 Tailless Agility Flight Research Aircraft
X-32 - The Boeing Joint Strike Fighter
X-35 - Progenitor to the F-35 Lightning II
X-45 Uninhabited Combat Air Vehicle
Into The Cauldron - The Lancaster MK.I Daylight Raid on Augsburg
Hurricane IIB Combat Log - 151 Wing RAF, North Russia 1941
RAF Meteor Jet Fighters in World War II, an Operational Log
Typhoon IA/B Combat Log - Operation Jubilee, August 1942
Defiant MK.I Combat Log - Fighter Command, May-September 1940
Blenheim MK.IF Combat Log - Fighter Command Day Fighter Sweeps/Night Interceptions, September 1939 - June 1940
Fortress MK.I Combat Log - Bomber Command High Altitude Bombing Operations, July-September 1941